Pendulum Craft

Pendulum Craft

Matthew Petchinsky

Pendulum Craft: A Complete Guide to Crafting and Using Personalized Divination Tools

By: Matthew Petchinsky

Introduction: The Art and Purpose of Pendulum Divination
Brief History of Pendulum Use in Divination

Pendulums have long been revered as tools for divination and spiritual guidance, bridging the mystical and the practical. Though pendulums are simple instruments at first glance—typically a weight suspended from a string or chain—their purpose and power are rich and layered. The earliest documented pendulum usage can be traced back to ancient Egypt, where healers used it to detect ailments and energy blockages within the body. Pendulums later became popular in the Middle Ages for dowsing, a technique that diviners used to locate water, minerals, or hidden objects. It was believed that by tapping into unseen energies, one could influence the pendulum's motion to reveal answers or guidance.

During the 17th and 18th centuries, the scientific community took an interest in pendulums, primarily for timekeeping, but the pendulum's connection to spiritual guidance and intuitive work continued to flourish among mystics and healers. This enduring appeal reflects humanity's desire to interact with forces beyond physical perception, using the pendulum as a bridge between the known and the unknown. Today, pendulums are a favored tool among diviners and spiritual practitioners worldwide, cherished for their simplicity, accessibility, and versatility.

Importance of Personalization in Pendulum Crafting

In the realm of divination, the most effective tools are those imbued with personal energy. Crafting a pendulum by hand allows you to create a piece that is uniquely attuned to your own intentions, energies, and needs. Many people find that using a store-bought pendulum lacks the same resonance or depth of connection as one they've crafted themselves. When you make your own pendulum, you choose the materials that resonate with you, whether they're crystals, metals, or personal artifacts. This personal connection enhances the pendulum's receptivity to your energy and makes it more responsive to your questions and guidance.

Personalized pendulums reflect their maker, often bearing symbolic elements that hold deep significance. For instance, choosing a rose quartz stone might reflect a desire to connect with energies of love and compassion, while a clear quartz crystal could indicate an interest in clarity and focus. Beyond the choice of materials, you can add other personal touches, such as engravings, symbolic charms, or color preferences, that deepen your connection with the tool. This customization can profoundly impact the accuracy of your readings, as the pendulum becomes a direct extension of your energy.

Overview of Pendulum Divination for Beginners

Pendulum divination, at its core, is a practice of tuning into the subconscious mind or a higher energetic plane to access answers that might otherwise remain elusive. For beginners, the practice can be an approachable introduction to divination as it requires minimal equipment and no extensive rituals. A pendulum is held by the user, typically between the thumb and forefinger, and allowed to swing freely. By asking questions and observing the direction of the pendulum's movements, practitioners interpret "yes" and "no" responses, with some adding further directional meanings based on their own interpretations.

This form of divination is also popular because it encourages personal intuition and allows the user to develop a deeper understanding of their own responses. Pendulums can be used for a range of purposes: answering simple yes-or-no questions, locating objects, assessing energy within a space, or even clarifying thoughts and emotions. By working with a pendulum, practitioners develop their ability to tune into subtle energies and enhance their intuitive skills. As you work with your pendulum, you'll learn to distinguish the subtle movements and signals it provides, building a practice that grows more insightful over time.

How This Guide Will Help You Craft and Connect with Your Own Pendulum

In this guide, you'll find a step-by-step approach to crafting a pendulum that is uniquely yours. From selecting materials to attuning and using your pendulum, each chapter is designed to support you in building a tool that feels deeply connected to your energy and purpose. You'll learn to choose the right crystals, metals, and additional elements that align with your intentions. Detailed crafting instructions will ensure you can bring your creative ideas to life, while advanced techniques will guide you in adding personal touches and symbolism that enhance the pendulum's resonance.

Beyond crafting, this guide will also lead you through the processes of cleansing, energizing, and connecting with your pendulum, allowing you to establish a reliable divination practice. We'll explore various ways to use your pendulum, from answering questions to assessing energy, and offer exercises to strengthen your intuition and deepen your connection with the tool. By the end of this journey, you will have a pendulum that is not only beautiful and functional but also an extension of your own unique energy and a powerful ally in your divination practice. This guide is both a creative endeavor and an invitation to explore the deeper insights that pendulum divination can offer.

Chapter 1: Understanding the Pendulum
The Basics of Pendulum Movement and Interpretation

At first glance, the pendulum may seem like a simple object—a weight on a string or chain. However, this humble tool holds the capacity to provide guidance, reveal hidden truths, and connect its user to a deeper source of wisdom. In divination, pendulums move in response to questions, offering insight through the direction and type of motion they exhibit. For beginners, the key to effective pendulum work lies in understanding the fundamental patterns of movement and how to interpret them.

Most practitioners observe that a pendulum moves in one of four primary ways:

1. **Vertical Swing (Up and Down):** Often interpreted as a "yes" response.
2. **Horizontal Swing (Side to Side):** Frequently taken to mean "no."
3. **Circular Motion (Clockwise or Counterclockwise):** This movement can signify openness or provide an indication of energetic flow, balance, or cleansing.
4. **Diagonal Movement:** Less common but may indicate indecision, lack of clarity, or a need for rephrasing the question.

To begin interpreting your pendulum's movements, it's essential to establish a personal language with it. Start by holding the pendulum in your hand, focusing on your breathing, and mentally connecting with it. Ask it simple, clear questions, such as "Show me yes" and "Show me no," and observe the motions. This initial practice helps you familiarize yourself with how your pendulum responds and builds a foundational language that will deepen with time and use.

Pendulum movements are subtle and may vary based on energy, location, and intention. Some practitioners prefer to "program" their pendulum by deciding beforehand what each motion means. Whether you choose to interpret responses intuitively or to assign specific meanings to each movement, consistency in your approach will improve accuracy over time. Experiment, pay attention, and trust that your pendulum's motion is reflecting both the question and your energy.

Energy and Intuition: How Pendulums Work

Pendulums operate on the principle of micro-movements—small, subconscious movements caused by the user's energy and intuition. The ideomotor effect, a psychological phenomenon where the body produces movements without conscious intention, is a scientific explanation for how pendulums respond. However, in spiritual terms, many practitioners believe that pendulums can also access energies beyond the physical, connecting the user to the wisdom of the subconscious mind or even to the energies of the universe.

Energy plays a central role in pendulum divination. When you hold a pendulum, your thoughts, emotions, and intentions influence the tool, prompting it to respond accordingly. This is why your emotional and mental state can affect the pendulum's accuracy. A clear, calm mind yields more reliable responses, while a cluttered or anxious mind can create confusing or erratic movements. It is beneficial to center yourself before each session, practicing meditation, deep breathing, or other calming techniques that help focus your mind and enhance your intuition.

Intuition is another crucial component of pendulum work. Rather than solely relying on rigid rules or interpretations, experienced diviners tune into their intuitive senses to discern deeper meanings in the pendulum's responses. Over time, you may find that your pendulum begins to respond more distinctly to your specific questions, reflecting your unique energy and intentions. In essence, the pendulum acts as an extension of your intuitive mind, translating subtle energies and unspoken knowledge into visible movement. Cultivating trust in your intuition will enable you to connect more deeply with your pendulum and access insights that extend beyond surface-level answers.

Choosing the Right Materials for Your Intention

The materials used to craft a pendulum have a profound effect on its energy and purpose. Each material resonates with specific qualities that influence the pendulum's responsiveness and accuracy. By choosing materials that align with your intentions, you can create a pendulum that is not only visually pleasing but also energetically attuned to your unique needs and goals.

1. **Crystals and Stones:** Crystals are a popular choice for pendulum weights because they carry distinct energies that amplify intentions. Different stones hold specific properties, which can enhance the pendulum's effectiveness:
    - **Amethyst:** Known for its calming energy, amethyst supports intuition, spiritual connection, and clarity of thought. It is ideal for those seeking answers related to inner wisdom, peace, or emotional healing.
    - **Rose Quartz:** Associated with love and compassion, rose quartz is often used in pendulums intended for questions about relationships, self-love, and emotional harmony.
    - **Clear Quartz:** Known as the "master healer," clear quartz enhances clarity, focus, and amplifies energy. This versatile stone can be used for a wide range of questions and purposes.
    - **Black Tourmaline or Obsidian:** For those looking to create a protective pendulum, black tourmaline or obsidian offers grounding and shielding qualities, ideal for cleansing or boundary-setting work.

2. Metals: Chains or cords made from specific metals can also impact the pendulum's energy:

- **Silver:** Known for its lunar and intuitive associations, silver is believed to enhance psychic abilities and is well-suited for divination work.
- **Copper:** Copper is a conductor of energy, making it an excellent choice for those who seek to amplify the pendulum's energetic reach. It is also grounding and balancing, often used in healing work.
- **Gold:** Gold is associated with abundance, warmth, and divine guidance, offering an energy of higher consciousness and spiritual insight.

2. **Natural Materials:** Some people prefer pendulums made from wood, bone, or other organic materials. These natural elements are grounding, connecting the user to earth energy and offering a sense of stability and balance. Wood pendulums are particularly cherished in shamanic practices and earth-based spirituality.

3. **Personal Items:** Incorporating a personal item, such as a meaningful charm, family heirloom, or object that holds sentimental value, can increase the pendulum's resonance with your energy. When using personal items, cleanse them before attachment to ensure that they hold only the energy you intend.

When selecting your materials, focus on what intuitively calls to you. Pay attention to any specific colors, shapes, or textures that feel significant, as these subtle inclinations often reflect what you need in your divination practice. By thoughtfully choosing each component, you craft a pendulum that is not only a tool but a deeply personal and energetically aligned companion.

With a solid understanding of pendulum movement, an appreciation of energy and intuition, and the knowledge to choose the right materials, you now have the foundational tools to begin your pendulum practice. The next chapter will guide you through the first steps of bringing your pendulum to life, from gathering materials to creating a simple yet powerful divination instrument.

Chapter 2: Selecting Materials

Creating a pendulum is a journey of both craftsmanship and intuition. The materials you select shape not only its aesthetic appeal but also its energetic properties and the depth of its connection to you. By choosing materials with intentionality, you infuse your pendulum with purpose and resonance, enhancing its ability to offer clear guidance. This chapter provides an in-depth look at various options for crafting a pendulum, including an exploration of different crystals, types of chains, and additional symbolic materials.

Overview of Different Crystals and Stones for Pendulums

Crystals and stones are the heart of many pendulums, cherished for their unique energies and metaphysical properties. Each crystal resonates with specific frequencies, which can enhance certain types of divination or connect to different aspects of the spiritual journey. Here's a look at some popular choices and their attributes:

1. **Amethyst**: Known for its calming, spiritual energy, amethyst aids in enhancing intuition, connecting with higher realms, and promoting emotional clarity. Amethyst pendulums are ideal for those seeking insights about inner peace, spiritual guidance, or healing.

2. **Rose Quartz**: A gentle stone associated with love, compassion, and self-acceptance, rose quartz is perfect for questions related to relationships, emotions, and self-healing. It is particularly useful for exploring matters of the heart and cultivating empathy.

3. **Clear Quartz**: Often called the "master healer," clear quartz is known for amplifying energy and intention. This versatile stone can be programmed for any purpose, making it a popular choice for all-purpose pendulums. It also enhances focus, making it ideal for clarity-based questions.

4. **Black Tourmaline**: Black tourmaline is a protective stone, grounding and shielding against negative energies. It is highly recommended for those who wish to use their pendulum in energy clearing work, boundary setting, or as a shield against unwanted influences.

5. **Citrine**: Known as the stone of abundance and manifestation, citrine carries vibrant, positive energy. Citrine pendulums are excellent for questions about prosperity, personal growth, and creativity. This stone is also believed to boost confidence and motivation.

6. **Selenite**: A stone of purification and high vibrational energy, selenite is used to connect with higher spiritual realms, angelic guidance, and cleansing practices. It is especially useful for those who use their pendulum for spiritual connection and want to keep it energetically clear.

7. **Lapis Lazuli**: Associated with wisdom, truth, and inner vision, lapis lazuli is used to access deeper insights and enhance spiritual awareness. This stone is ideal for pendulums focused on self-discovery, communication, and knowledge-seeking.

8. **Obsidian**: A grounding and protective stone, obsidian is associated with shadow work and introspection. Obsidian pendulums are often used in divination that involves deep self-reflection, healing trauma, and exploring subconscious patterns.

These are just a few examples, but many other stones carry unique energies and can be used effectively in pendulums. Choose a crystal that resonates with your current needs or goals, allowing its properties to guide you toward the clarity and answers you seek.

Types of Chains, Cords, and Strings

The material you use to suspend the pendulum can also influence its movement, comfort, and symbolic meaning. Chains, cords, and strings each have distinct qualities, and selecting the right one will enhance both the functionality and energy of your pendulum.

1. **Metal Chains**: Metal chains are durable, practical, and often preferred for their stable movement. Chains allow the pendulum to swing smoothly without tangling or catching, making them ideal for precise divination work. Each type of metal holds specific qualities:
    - **Silver**: Associated with lunar energy, intuition, and psychic abilities. Silver chains are perfect for pendulums used in spiritual or intuitive work.
    - **Copper**: Known as an energy amplifier and conductor, copper is a popular choice for those who want their pendulum to be energetically vibrant and responsive. It also carries a grounding quality.
    - **Gold**: Symbolizing abundance, wisdom, and divine insight, gold chains can add a sense of spiritual elegance and power to your pendulum. It is often chosen for divination related to wealth or higher wisdom.
2. **Natural Cords**: Cotton, hemp, or silk cords offer an organic, earthy feel. Natural cords connect you to grounded energies, making them suitable for individuals who practice nature-based spirituality or seek to connect with earth energies. They're also ideal for pendulums used in personal or healing work, as they're softer and feel more personal.
3. **Leather or Suede Strings**: Leather cords are durable, flexible, and carry grounding, stabilizing energy. Leather is often chosen by those who seek a raw, natural look and feel, or who connect with shamanic or ancestral practices. However, because leather is an animal product, it may not be preferred by everyone.

4. **Beaded or Woven Strings**: Some pendulums are crafted with beaded strings, allowing additional customization and energy alignment. Beads of different colors or materials can add symbolic meaning to the pendulum, such as incorporating chakra colors for balance or specific crystals for added intention.

The length of the chain or cord should be comfortable for holding and swinging, usually around 6-8 inches. If you prefer your pendulum to have a strong, grounded swing, opt for a metal chain; if you'd like a more personal or tactile connection, a natural cord or leather may be better suited to your intentions.

Symbolism and Properties of Various Materials

Each material in your pendulum, from the weight to the chain, can carry symbolic meaning and intention. Here's how different materials contribute to a pendulum's overall purpose and energy:

- **Crystals and Stones**: Represent the element of earth and often carry energies aligned with healing, insight, protection, or amplification.
- **Metals**: Often associated with alchemical symbolism and connected to planets. For example, silver is linked with the moon and intuition, while gold is associated with the sun, abundance, and wisdom.
- **Organic Materials (Wood, Bone, Shells)**: These elements connect the pendulum to nature, ancestry, and grounding energies. Pendulums with organic materials are often used for personal insights, grounding practices, and connecting with earth-based energies.
- **Colors**: Color symbolism can be integrated into the pendulum's design to align with specific energies:
    - **Red**: Passion, grounding, and vitality
    - **Blue**: Communication, calm, and spiritual insight
    - **Green**: Healing, growth, and abundance

- ◦ **Purple**: Spirituality, intuition, and higher consciousness
- ◦ **White/Clear**: Purity, clarity, and universal energy
- ◦ **Black**: Protection, mystery, and grounding

Understanding the symbolism behind each material allows you to infuse deeper meaning into your pendulum. The more thought and care you put into each selection, the more resonant and personalized your pendulum will become.

How to Choose Materials That Resonate with You

Choosing materials for your pendulum is an intuitive process. Begin by reflecting on your primary intention for the pendulum. Are you seeking guidance on a specific area of life, such as love, career, or spirituality? Or are you drawn to pendulum work for energy clearing, self-discovery, or connection with nature? Aligning your choices with your intention will guide you toward the materials best suited to your needs.

Here are some tips for selecting materials that resonate personally:

1. **Follow Your Intuition**: Often, your subconscious knows what resonates with you. Pay attention to which crystals, colors, or materials you feel drawn to without overthinking. These instinctive choices usually reveal what you need.

2. **Reflect on Your Current Goals**: Consider what you hope to achieve or gain clarity on through pendulum divination. For instance, if you seek emotional healing, a rose quartz pendulum with a silver chain might feel ideal. If your focus is protection, a black tourmaline with a copper chain could suit your needs.

3. **Experiment with Touch and Feel**: If you have access to a variety of crystals and materials, hold them and see how they feel in your hand. Some stones or chains may resonate more strongly, providing a sense of warmth, calm, or clarity.

4. **Consider Your Lifestyle and Practice**: If you plan to carry the pendulum regularly or use it in specific environments, consider practical factors. For example, a durable chain might be better

suited for outdoor use, while a delicate silk cord may work best for home practices.

5. **Trust the Process**: Sometimes, you may feel a connection with materials that don't initially seem relevant to your intention. Trust that your intuition is guiding you, and allow the materials to choose you as much as you choose them.

By combining thoughtful selection with intuitive guidance, you create a pendulum that is not only a divination tool but also an extension of your personal energy and intention. Once your materials are chosen, the next chapter will guide you through the process of assembling and crafting your pendulum, bringing your vision to life and infusing it with purpose.

Chapter 3: Crafting a Simple Pendulum

Creating a pendulum is both an artistic and spiritual process. The act of crafting your own pendulum allows you to imbue it with your unique energy and intentions, creating a tool that is deeply personal and attuned to your needs. This chapter provides a step-by-step guide to creating a basic pendulum, discusses common challenges, and offers techniques for balancing and calibrating your pendulum to ensure optimal performance.

Step-by-Step Guide to Creating a Basic Pendulum

Creating a basic pendulum involves assembling a weight (typically a crystal, stone, or other small object) and attaching it to a chain, cord, or string that allows it to swing freely. Here is a step-by-step guide to crafting a simple yet powerful pendulum:

1. **Gather Your Materials**:
     - **Weight (Crystal or Stone)**: Choose a crystal or stone that resonates with you. The size should be comfortable to hold, not too heavy, and preferably with a pointed end for better motion and focus.
     - **Chain, Cord, or String**: Select a chain or cord approximately 6-8 inches long, depending on your preference. The chain should allow the weight to swing freely and should feel comfortable in your hand.
     - **Jump Ring or Attachment**: This is optional but helpful, especially if you're using a crystal or stone with a drilled hole or setting. A small jump ring or metal attachment can make it easier to secure the weight to the chain.
     - **Optional Bead or Spacer**: A small bead or spacer at the top of the chain can enhance grip and stability and add a personal touch to the design.

2. Prepare Your Crystal or Stone:

- If you're using a crystal with a drilled hole, simply slide the chain or cord through the hole.
- If the crystal does not have a hole, wrap a piece of wire around it securely, leaving a loop at the top to attach it to the chain.
- Another option is to use a small metal cap with adhesive, which provides a secure way to attach the stone to the chain.

2. Attach the Weight to the Chain:

- Using pliers, attach the jump ring to the top of the weight or crystal and then loop it through the end of the chain.
- If your chain does not have a jump ring, tie the cord or chain securely to the stone or crystal.
- Check the connection to ensure it is secure and that the pendulum swings freely without any obstruction.

3. Create a Grip Point:

- For ease of use, many pendulums include a small bead or charm at the top of the chain where your fingers will hold it. This makes it more comfortable to use and can also add a decorative touch.
- Secure the bead or charm with a knot or attach it to the end of the chain using a jump ring.

4. Test the Pendulum's Movement:

- Hold your pendulum by the chain, allowing the weight to hang freely.
- Check that it moves smoothly and that the chain or cord does not cause any restriction.
- Adjust any part that feels too tight or too loose, ensuring a balanced and responsive swing.

5. **Cleansing and Energizing the Pendulum**:
    - Before using your pendulum, cleanse it to remove any residual energies from materials or handling. Popular methods include smudging with sage or palo santo, placing it in moonlight overnight, or using sound (such as a bell or singing bowl).
    - Hold the pendulum in your hands, close your eyes, and focus on infusing it with your energy and intentions. Visualize it as an extension of yourself, attuned to your questions and guidance.

Common Challenges and Solutions

As with any craft, creating a pendulum may involve a few challenges. Here are some common issues and solutions to help you complete your project successfully:

1. **Unstable Swing or Off-Balance Movement**:
    - **Solution**: This often happens if the weight is not centered or if the chain is too tight. Check that the weight is evenly balanced, and make any adjustments necessary to center it. If using a cord, ensure it isn't twisted.
2. **Chain or Cord is Too Short or Too Long**:
    - **Solution**: Ideally, the chain should be around 6-8 inches, but it depends on your preference. If the chain is too long, trim it to a comfortable length. If it's too short, consider adding an extender or switching to a longer chain or cord.
3. **Crystal or Weight Falls Off**:
    - **Solution**: If your weight or crystal detaches, make sure to use a strong adhesive for glue-on caps or ensure that the wire wrapping is secure. Double-check jump rings and attachments, especially if you plan on frequent use.
4. **Difficulty in Attaching the Weight to the Chain**:
    - **Solution**: Some stones are more challenging to attach due to their shape or size. Experiment with different attachment methods, such as wire wrapping or using a cap with adhesive. Jewelry-making supplies like clasps, jump rings, or bail beads can simplify the process.
5. **Tangling or Knotting of Cord**:
    - **Solution**: This is common with natural cords, such as hemp or cotton. Consider using a chain if tangling is an

issue, or lightly wax the cord to reduce twisting and knotting.

6. **Inconsistent Swing in Divination**:
    - **Solution**: If the pendulum's movement seems erratic, it may need cleansing or re-energizing. Take time to center yourself, and cleanse the pendulum using your preferred method. Often, erratic movement is a result of accumulated energy or your own unfocused energy.

Techniques for Balancing and Calibrating Your Pendulum

Once your pendulum is crafted, balancing and calibrating it will ensure that it moves smoothly and responds accurately to your energy and intentions. Here are steps to properly calibrate your pendulum:

1. **Initial Balancing Test**:
    - Hold the pendulum by its chain or cord, keeping your hand as steady as possible.
    - Observe its natural swing. If it seems to move erratically or doesn't settle into a smooth motion, check that the weight is attached securely and that the chain is untangled and centered.

2. **Determine Your Personal "Yes" and "No" Responses**:
    - Every pendulum responds uniquely to its user, so calibrate it by establishing your personal response signals. Ask it simple, clear questions to determine its movements for "yes" and "no" answers.
    - A common approach is to hold the pendulum and say, "Show me yes." Observe the direction in which it moves—whether vertically, horizontally, or in a circle.

    ◦ Repeat with "Show me no." Once you identify these movements, you'll have a foundational response pattern for future questions.

3. **Create a Neutral Position**:
    ◦ Before beginning each session, establish a "neutral" or "resting" position for your pendulum. This allows the pendulum to reset between questions, ensuring that it isn't influenced by previous responses.
    ◦ To do this, simply hold the pendulum steady, focus on taking a few deep breaths, and mentally clear any residual energy from previous sessions.

4. **Re-Calibrate as Needed**:
    ◦ Over time, your pendulum may need recalibration, especially if you notice shifts in its response patterns. Repeating the "Show me yes" and "Show me no" exercises can keep the pendulum attuned to your energy.
    ◦ Recalibrate regularly, especially if you use your pendulum often or for different types of questions.

5. **Practice Consistency in Holding Technique**:
    ◦ Hold your pendulum in the same way each time for consistency in readings. Most people hold the chain between the thumb and forefinger, allowing the pendulum to swing freely. Avoid clutching too tightly, as it can disrupt the pendulum's natural motion.

6. **Clear and Focus Before Each Use**:
    ◦ Before each use, take a moment to clear your mind and focus on your intention. By centering yourself, you create an energetic environment that supports accurate and clear responses.

Creating your own pendulum and ensuring it is balanced and calibrated is a meaningful part of establishing a reliable divination tool. This chapter has guided you through the essential steps of crafting a pendulum, overcoming common challenges, and calibrating it to reflect your unique energy. Now that your pendulum is ready, the next chapter will cover advanced crafting techniques for adding symbolic elements and enhancing the pendulum's spiritual resonance, helping you create a tool that aligns even more deeply with your intentions.

Chapter 4: Advanced Crafting Techniques

Once you've mastered the basics of pendulum creation, you may feel called to explore advanced crafting techniques to make your pendulum more unique and energetically resonant. Advanced techniques allow you to infuse your pendulum with deeper meaning, making it a highly personalized tool that reflects your individual journey and intentions. This chapter will explore techniques like using multiple stones or charms, adding symbolic engravings, experimenting with unique shapes, and incorporating personal items for added energy. Each technique provides an opportunity to create a pendulum that is not only functional but also a profound representation of your spirit.

Using Multiple Stones or Charms

Adding multiple stones or charms to your pendulum enhances its versatility and energy by incorporating various properties and intentions into one tool. Whether you aim to balance multiple energies or connect with diverse aspects of your life, using multiple stones or charms can expand your pendulum's capacity for divination.

1. **Selecting Complementary Stones**:
    - When using multiple stones, consider the qualities of each and how they work together. For instance, pairing **amethyst** (intuition and spirituality) with **rose quartz** (love and compassion) can create a pendulum that helps answer questions about relationships with a spiritual focus.
    - Some effective combinations include:
        - **Clear Quartz and Black Tourmaline**: Clarity and protection, balancing positive and grounding energies.
        - **Lapis Lazuli and Citrine**: Insight and abundance, aligning wisdom with prosperity.

- **Moonstone and Sunstone**: Balance of feminine and masculine energies, representing the lunar and solar influences.

2. **Creating a "Stacked" or "Cluster" Design**:
   - In a stacked design, stones of different shapes and sizes are layered, usually in descending order. This allows the energy to flow from one stone to the next, creating a layered effect. For example, you could start with a small, grounding stone like hematite at the top and end with a larger, intuition-focused stone like amethyst.
   - Cluster designs group multiple small stones or charms around a central stone. This arrangement provides a balanced energy, allowing each stone to contribute equally to the pendulum's overall power.

3. **Adding Charms for Symbolic Enhancement**:
   - Charms can add specific meanings and amplify the pendulum's purpose. For example:
     - **Ankh**: Symbol of life and vitality, ideal for health or wellness-focused divination.
     - **Crescent Moon**: Associated with intuition, dreams, and feminine energy, suitable for spiritual questions.
     - **Feather**: Represents freedom, spirituality, and communication, perfect for questions about direction or guidance.

4. **Balancing Multiple Stones and Charms**:
   - When adding multiple elements, balance the weight so the pendulum swings freely. Place larger stones or charms at the bottom, with smaller elements higher on the chain to ensure even movement.
   - Test the pendulum's swing after adding each element to make any necessary adjustments.

Adding Symbolic Elements or Engravings

Symbols and engravings add a layer of meaning to your pendulum, personalizing it with imagery or words that align with your spiritual path or divination goals. Adding these elements requires some craftsmanship, but they can make your pendulum more meaningful and attuned to your unique practice.

1. **Choosing Symbols with Personal Significance:**
   - Symbols are powerful tools in connecting to specific energies, deities, or spiritual paths. For example:
     - **The Tree of Life**: Represents growth, connection, and wisdom, suitable for those seeking life guidance or ancestral connection.
     - **Runes**: Each rune has a unique meaning and can be engraved or painted onto a metal or wood part of the pendulum to invoke specific energies, such as protection (Algiz) or insight (Ansuz).
     - **Astrological Signs**: Engraving your sun, moon, or rising sign on the pendulum connects it to your astrological identity, adding a celestial focus.
2. **Incorporating Sacred Geometry:**
   - Geometric patterns like the **Flower of Life**, **Metatron's Cube**, or **pentagram** can be engraved on the pendulum to symbolize universal truths and sacred knowledge. Sacred geometry enhances the pendulum's connection to the cosmos and aligns it with the laws of nature.

- You can engrave these patterns on metal components or paint them on a wooden base for subtle yet powerful effects.

3. **Engraving Techniques**:
    - **Metal Engraving**: For metal pendulums, use an engraving tool or etching pen. If you're new to engraving, practice on a spare piece before working on your pendulum.
    - **Wood Burning**: For wooden pendulums, use a wood-burning tool to inscribe symbols. Wood burning adds warmth and an earthy quality, connecting the pendulum to nature.
    - **Crystal Etching**: Some stones, such as clear quartz, can be etched carefully with diamond-tip tools. Crystal etching requires precision, so only attempt this if you're comfortable with fine tools and delicate materials.

4. **Adding Inspirational Words or Affirmations**:
    - You can engrave or paint affirmations, such as "Peace," "Truth," or "Guidance," onto your pendulum. These words serve as reminders of your intention each time you use the pendulum and help amplify your focus.

Creating Pendulums with Unique Shapes or Designs

Experimenting with shapes and designs can elevate your pendulum's functionality and aesthetic, allowing you to create a truly one-of-a-kind divination tool. Different shapes channel energy in distinct ways and can deepen your connection with the pendulum.

1. **Exploring Unique Shapes**:
   - **Pointed Crystals**: Crystal points, especially double-terminated ones, focus and direct energy clearly. These are ideal for focused questions or when you seek precise answers.
   - **Teardrop Shapes**: Teardrop pendulums often have a soothing, emotional quality, aligning well with questions of love, healing, and emotional balance.
   - **Sphere Pendulums**: Spheres represent wholeness and balance, making them suitable for broad or open-ended questions. Spheres also swing smoothly and are known for creating a calming energy.
   - **Pendulums with Spiral Design**: Some pendulums feature spirals or corkscrew designs, enhancing energy flow and aligning with transformational or cleansing work.
2. **Using Geometric Shapes for Intentions**:
   - **Hexagon**: Represents balance and harmony; ideal for pendulums focused on personal well-being or relationship harmony.
   - **Triangle**: Represents transformation, action, and manifestation. Pendulums with a triangular component can be particularly effective for questions related to growth, change, or new ventures.
3. **Adding Artisanal Touches with Color or Paint**:
   - Paint designs or symbols onto your pendulum to customize its appearance further. You can use watercolor for a delicate, ethereal look or acrylic paint for more vibrant designs. Choose colors that resonate with specific energies:

blue for communication, green for healing, or purple for spirituality.

Incorporating Personal Items for Added Energy

Infusing your pendulum with a piece of personal significance, such as a family heirloom, a meaningful charm, or an object that holds sentimental value, can create a deeply resonant tool that strengthens your connection to it.

1. **Choosing Items with Meaning:**
   - Select items that hold positive memories, intentions, or energies. Examples include a small charm from a family member, a piece of jewelry with sentimental value, or a natural item like a feather, seashell, or stone you've collected from a meaningful location.
   - Ensure that the item is compatible in size and weight to allow for smooth pendulum movement.
2. **Attaching Personal Items:**
   - You can incorporate personal items in several ways:
     - **Adding a Personal Charm to the Chain**: Attach the charm to the top or bottom of the chain, depending on your preference. A charm at the top adds a personal grip point, while a charm at the bottom integrates with the primary weight.
     - **Securing Inside a Crystal Cage**: Some pendulums come with a crystal cage, where small items or additional stones can be placed. This allows you to change out personal items over time if you wish.
     - **Embedding Items in Resin Pendulums**: If you're comfortable working with resin, you can create a custom resin pendulum with small personal items embedded inside, such as tiny stones, pieces of paper with affirmations, or small feathers. Resin crafting

allows for significant customization and can capture meaningful elements within a durable pendulum.

3. **Blessing and Energizing Personal Items**:
   ◦ Before adding a personal item, cleanse and bless it to remove any stagnant or conflicting energies. Hold it in your hands, focusing on infusing it with positive energy and intentions. Visualize the item blending with the pendulum's energy, amplifying its strength and purpose.
   ◦ You might choose to perform a simple ritual where you place both the pendulum and personal item on an altar, light a candle, and set an intention for them to work harmoniously together.

Advanced crafting techniques allow you to create a pendulum that is much more than a divination tool—it becomes a unique expression of your personal journey, intentions, and energy. By combining multiple stones, incorporating symbolic elements, exploring unique shapes, and adding personal items, you create a pendulum that resonates deeply with you and enhances your practice. These techniques not only expand your skills as a crafter but also deepen your connection with the pendulum as a powerful guide and ally on your spiritual path. The next chapter will guide you in energizing and attuning your pendulum, preparing it for its role as a responsive, reliable tool for divination.

Chapter 5: Enhancing and Activating Your Pendulum

Now that you've crafted your pendulum, the next step is to prepare it for use by enhancing and activating its energy. This process involves cleansing, energizing, and attuning the pendulum to align with your energy. By dedicating time to these steps, you build a stronger, more responsive connection, allowing the pendulum to become a reliable tool in your divination practice. This chapter covers various methods for cleansing and energizing your pendulum, rituals for attunement, and tips for practicing initial readings to develop a personal connection with your new tool.

Methods for Cleansing and Energizing New Pendulums

Every pendulum absorbs energy from its environment and from those who handle it. Cleansing your pendulum removes any residual or stagnant energy, creating a clear and receptive tool for divination. Once cleansed, energizing the pendulum ensures that it's aligned with your intentions and is ready for accurate use.

1. **Water Cleansing (for Waterproof Stones and Metals):**
    - **Method**: Hold your pendulum under a gentle stream of running water (such as a natural stream or faucet), imagining the water washing away any unwanted energy. Alternatively, place it in a bowl of purified water.
    - **Precautions**: Avoid water cleansing for stones that are water-sensitive, like selenite or malachite, as these can be damaged by moisture. Ensure that any metal parts are also waterproof.
    - **Duration**: Cleanse under running water for 1-2 minutes, or in a bowl of water for about 10 minutes.
2. **Salt Cleansing:**
    - **Method**: Place your pendulum in a bowl of sea salt, which absorbs unwanted energy. Alternatively, place the pendu-

lum on a bed of salt to avoid any direct contact with potentially sensitive materials.

- ◦ **Precautions**: Avoid this method if your pendulum contains softer stones or metals that may react with salt.
- ◦ **Duration**: Leave the pendulum in the salt for a few hours or overnight, then dispose of the salt afterward.

3. **Smoke Cleansing (Smudging)**:
   - ◦ **Method**: Use sacred herbs like sage, palo santo, or cedar. Light the herb bundle and pass your pendulum through the smoke, visualizing it being purified and reset.
   - ◦ **Ideal For**: This is a gentle method suitable for all types of stones and materials. It's also ideal for people who want to incorporate ritual and intention into the cleansing process.
   - ◦ **Duration**: Pass the pendulum through the smoke for 1-3 minutes.

4. **Sound Cleansing**:
   - ◦ **Method**: Sound vibrations can cleanse and balance your pendulum effectively. Use a singing bowl, tuning fork, bell, or even vocal chanting to produce a resonant sound, holding the pendulum close to the sound source.
   - ◦ **Ideal For**: Sound cleansing works for all pendulums and is especially beneficial for energetically sensitive crystals.
   - ◦ **Duration**: Cleanse for 1-3 minutes or until you feel the energy has shifted.

5. **Sun and Moonlight Charging**:
   - ◦ **Method**: Place your pendulum outside or on a windowsill where it can absorb the sun's or moon's light. Sunlight energizes with warmth and vitality, while moonlight infuses gentle, intuitive energy.
   - ◦ **Precautions**: Be cautious with sunlight exposure, as some stones (like amethyst) may fade with prolonged sunlight.
   - ◦ **Duration**: 1-2 hours for sunlight, or overnight for moonlight, especially during the full moon for maximum energy.

6. **Crystal Charging**:
   - **Method**: Place your pendulum on a larger crystal or crystal cluster, such as selenite or clear quartz, which naturally cleanse and amplify energy.
   - **Ideal For**: This is a subtle yet powerful method suitable for any pendulum. Selenite is particularly effective for gentle, continuous cleansing and recharging.
   - **Duration**: Leave the pendulum on the crystal for several hours or overnight.

Once you have cleansed your pendulum, take a moment to hold it and visualize it as clear, refreshed, and ready for your use. The next step is energizing, where you infuse it with your intentions and focus, charging it for divination.

Rituals for Attuning the Pendulum to Your Energy

Attuning the pendulum connects it directly to your energy, ensuring that it becomes an extension of your intuition. Attuning is especially important for new pendulums, as it aligns their energetic frequency with yours, making them more responsive to your questions and guidance.

1. **Meditation Ritual for Attunement**:
   - **Preparation**: Find a quiet space where you can sit undisturbed. Hold the pendulum in your dominant hand, close your eyes, and focus on your breath.
   - **Visualization**: Visualize a beam of light surrounding you and your pendulum, connecting the two of you. Imagine this light filling the pendulum with your energy, infusing it with trust, clarity, and purpose.
   - **Affirmation**: As you hold the pendulum, mentally or verbally affirm, "This pendulum is attuned to my energy. It will guide me with truth and clarity."
   - **Duration**: Meditate with this visualization for 5-10 minutes, or until you feel a sense of connection.

2. **Naming and Bonding Ritual**:
   - Some practitioners choose to give their pendulums a name, a practice that creates a more personal relationship with the tool. This can be a meaningful way to honor your pendulum as an ally in divination.
   - **Method**: Once named, speak to the pendulum directly. Hold it close to your heart, and say its name, followed by an intention such as, "May you be a clear and honest guide, revealing only what serves my highest good."

3. **Holding and Infusion Ritual**:
   - After cleansing, hold the pendulum in your hands, one hand cupped over the other, and close your eyes.

- **Intention Setting**: Focus on the purpose for which you intend to use the pendulum, whether for guidance, protection, healing, or clarity.
- **Energy Transfer**: Imagine energy flowing from your heart center, down your arms, and into the pendulum. Feel the warmth in your hands as it absorbs your energy.
- **Duration**: Continue for 3-5 minutes, or until you feel a sense of unity with the pendulum.

4. **Daily Attunement Practice**:
   - For the first few days of working with a new pendulum, spend a few minutes each day holding and focusing on your intention. This daily ritual will reinforce your connection and improve the pendulum's responsiveness.

By completing these attunement rituals, you solidify a bond between yourself and the pendulum, preparing it to become an intuitive guide in your divination work.

Practicing Initial Readings and Building a Connection

Now that your pendulum is cleansed, energized, and attuned, the next step is to practice using it to build a reliable connection. Initial readings are essential for establishing a "language" with your pendulum, allowing it to respond consistently to your questions.

1. **Establishing Yes, No, and Neutral Responses**:
   - Begin by holding the pendulum over a flat surface, allowing it to hang still. Ask it to "Show me yes." Observe the direction it swings, whether vertically, horizontally, or in a circular motion.
   - Next, ask it to "Show me no" and note the movement.
   - Finally, ask it to "Show me neutral," which can serve as a resting or undecided response.

- **Tip**: Repeat these questions until you consistently see the same movements for each response.

2. **Testing with Known Questions**:
   - To confirm the accuracy of the pendulum's responses, ask it simple yes/no questions to which you already know the answer, such as "Is my name ___?" or "Is today Tuesday?" This will help validate its initial responses.
   - If the pendulum's responses are inconsistent, pause, take a few deep breaths, and refocus. Consistency will improve with practice.

3. **Asking Open-Ended Questions**:
   - Move on to questions that are more open-ended but not emotionally charged. For example, ask questions like, "Is this a good day for meditation?" or "Should I spend time in nature today?"
   - Observe the pendulum's response and reflect on whether it resonates with you. Practicing with neutral, low-stakes questions helps build trust in the tool's accuracy.

4. **Daily Connection Practice**:
   - Spend a few minutes each day holding the pendulum and asking basic questions. This daily practice strengthens the connection and helps you become more attuned to its movements.
   - Take note of any changes or shifts in its responsiveness, as well as any patterns in its motion that might provide insights into your own energy and intuition.

5. **Journaling Observations**:
   - Keep a journal to document your pendulum's responses, any notable patterns, and reflections on its accuracy. Over time, you may notice trends that enhance your understanding and deepen your connection with the pendulum.

- ◦ This practice is particularly helpful if you use the pendulum for different areas of life, as it allows you to see how it responds across various subjects and intentions.

6. **Building Trust Through Consistency**:
   - ◦ Developing a reliable connection with your pendulum requires consistent practice. Approach each session with a calm and open mind, and trust in the pendulum's ability to guide you.

By following these steps to cleanse, energize, attune, and practice with your pendulum, you are preparing it to become a trusted ally in your divination practice. Each of these steps strengthens the bond between you and the pendulum, ensuring that it responds to you with clarity and precision. The next chapter will explore using your pendulum for specific types of divination and provide guidance on interpreting its responses in a variety of contexts.

Chapter 6: Pendulum Boards and Mats

Pendulum boards and mats are powerful accessories that enhance the divination experience, offering a structured surface with markings to guide the pendulum's responses. Creating a custom board or mat allows you to infuse your divination practice with personal symbolism and intention, providing clarity and focus to each reading. In this chapter, you will learn how to design your own divination board or mat, explore different layouts for specific types of questions, and gain tips on crafting portable and reversible boards to suit various divination needs.

Designing Your Own Divination Board or Mat

Creating a pendulum board or mat is an opportunity to add both functionality and artistry to your divination practice. A personalized board can feature markings that align with your spiritual symbols, preferred colors, or question types, helping to enhance your connection to your pendulum and improve the accuracy of your readings.

1. **Choosing Your Board or Mat Base:**
   - **Materials**: You can create your pendulum board from a variety of materials, including wood, acrylic, fabric, or even paper. Each material has its own benefits:
     - **Wood**: Durable and grounding, wood is ideal for those who want a sturdy, long-lasting board. Wood also allows for painting or wood burning, making it highly customizable.
     - **Acrylic or Glass**: These materials are smooth and easy to clean, ideal for creating polished, modern-looking boards. Acrylic is also suitable for adding intricate designs with paint markers.
     - **Fabric or Felt**: If you prefer a portable option, fabric mats are lightweight, easy to roll up, and can be decorated with fabric paint or sewn symbols.

- **Size**: Choose a size that's comfortable for your space and purpose. Smaller boards are convenient for travel, while larger boards offer more room for detailed layouts.

2. **Selecting Your Colors and Symbolism**:
    - **Colors**: Colors carry symbolic meanings that can add depth to your divination. For example, purple enhances intuition, blue encourages communication, and green supports healing and growth. Consider the color's meaning and how it complements the type of readings you plan to do.
    - **Symbols**: Adding personal symbols—such as sacred geometry, runes, astrological signs, or natural elements (e.g., sun, moon, or tree)—can enhance your connection to the board. Choose symbols that resonate with you spiritually or align with your pendulum's purpose.

3. **Basic Layout Elements**:
    - **Yes/No/Maybe**: The most common layout includes markings for "Yes," "No," and "Maybe," placed at different points on the board. These sections are often located at the top, bottom, and sides of the board.
    - **Directional Compass**: Adding a compass rose (north, south, east, west) can help in readings related to travel, decisions, or finding lost items.
    - **Alphabet and Numbers**: For more complex questions, you can include the alphabet or numbers around the edges of the board, allowing your pendulum to spell out words or indicate specific dates or quantities.

4. **Decorative Touches and Details**:
    - Add decorative flourishes, like borders, patterns, or metallic paint accents, to make the board aesthetically pleasing and inviting.

○ You may also want to inscribe a personal affirmation, such as "Guided by Truth" or "In Alignment with My Higher Self," to help set the tone for each reading.

5. **Finalizing and Sealing Your Board**:

   ○ Once your board design is complete, you may wish to seal it with a clear varnish or protective spray, particularly if you've painted on wood or used permanent markers on acrylic. This layer protects the design and keeps your board in good condition for long-term use.

Different Layouts for Specific Questions

The layout of your pendulum board can be customized to serve different types of questions, giving your pendulum specific points to swing toward for clarity and detail. Below are several layout ideas for various divination needs:

1. **Basic Yes/No/Maybe Layout**:

   ○ **Design**: Divide the board into three primary sections labeled "Yes," "No," and "Maybe." Position "Yes" at the top, "No" at the bottom, and "Maybe" to the side.

   ○ **Usage**: This layout is simple and effective for straightforward yes/no questions. It's ideal for beginners or when seeking clarity on basic decisions.

2. **Compass Rose Layout**:

   ○ **Design**: Draw a compass rose with directions (north, south, east, and west) at the edges, and add "Yes" and "No" markers in the top and bottom corners.

   ○ **Usage**: This layout is useful for readings related to directions, travel, or choosing a physical location. For example, if you're seeking clarity on the direction to take in life, your pendulum can indicate a cardinal direction.

3. **Astrological and Elemental Layout**:
    - **Design**: Divide the board into 12 sections, representing the zodiac signs, and add symbols for the four elements (fire, water, air, earth) in the center.
    - **Usage**: This layout is excellent for readings connected to astrology, such as identifying astrological influences, timing events, or aligning with specific planetary energies. The elements in the center can indicate which elemental energies are at play in the reading.

4. **Alphabet and Number Layout**:
    - **Design**: Place the alphabet in a semicircle or full circle around the edge of the board, with numbers 0–9 below.
    - **Usage**: This layout is suitable for more detailed readings, especially for asking for names, places, or dates. It allows the pendulum to spell out words or indicate specific quantities, making it a versatile choice for complex questions.

5. **Chakra and Body Energy Layout**:
    - **Design**: Mark the board with symbols for each of the seven chakras (root, sacral, solar plexus, heart, throat, third eye, and crown) in a line or circle, and add additional markers for "Blocked," "Balanced," and "Needs Attention."
    - **Usage**: This layout is specifically for energy readings. It allows you to ask the pendulum about the status of each chakra or energy center, assessing which areas of your body or spirit may need healing or focus.

6. **Yes/No/Uncertain with Time Indicators**:
    - **Design**: Along with "Yes" and "No" markers, add segments labeled with "Soon," "Later," "Within a Year," or "Undetermined."
    - **Usage**: This layout is helpful for timing questions, allowing the pendulum to indicate when an event may occur in addition to giving a yes/no answer.

Experiment with these layouts to see which works best for your needs. As you gain experience, you may find that some layouts resonate more deeply, depending on the type of question or divination goal.

Crafting Portable or Reversible Boards

If you like to conduct pendulum readings in different locations or travel frequently, a portable or reversible board can be a valuable addition to your divination toolkit. Here are some tips on creating boards that are easy to transport and serve multiple functions.

1. **Creating a Fabric Pendulum Mat**:
   - **Material**: Use sturdy fabric, like canvas, felt, or velvet, that's durable yet flexible enough to roll or fold.
   - **Design**: Paint or embroider your layout onto the fabric. Fabric markers and fabric paint work well for adding details that will withstand wear.
   - **Portability**: Roll up the mat when not in use, and secure it with a ribbon or elastic band for easy transport. A fabric mat is also lightweight, making it perfect for travel or outdoor readings.
2. **Double-Sided or Reversible Boards**:
   - **Materials**: Use materials like wood or acrylic that can be designed on both sides. Paint one side with a basic yes/no layout and the other with an alphabet or directional layout.
   - **Design Consideration**: Ensure that each side has a durable, sealed finish to prevent designs from wearing off with use. You can apply a clear varnish or lacquer to each side to protect the board's integrity.
   - **Usage**: Having multiple layouts on a single board allows you to switch between them based on the question type, without needing multiple boards.
3. **Magnetic or Foldable Pendulum Boards**:
   - **Materials**: Consider using a magnetic surface or attaching magnetic symbols. You can place markers for "Yes," "No,"

"Maybe," and other segments on the board, rearranging them as needed.

- **Portability**: Foldable boards can be made by scoring a thin wooden or acrylic board and attaching a hinge in the middle. This allows it to fold in half, making it easier to store and transport.
- **Customization**: Magnetic layouts give you the flexibility to change the layout according to your divination goals, offering a highly adaptable option.

4. **Travel-Size Pendulum Boards**:
- **Materials**: Use a small wooden plaque, acrylic square, or durable cardboard. Decorate with a miniature version of your preferred layout.
- **Portability**: This board can fit in a small bag or pouch, making it easy to carry with your pendulum. You can even create a pocket-sized fabric mat that folds neatly into your wallet or bag.
- **Design Tips**: Keep the layout simple, as the space will be limited. Stick to a basic yes/no and maybe design or a single directional layout.

5. **Using Protective Pouches or Cases**:
- Whether you're using a fabric mat or a hard board, consider storing it in a protective pouch or case when traveling. Fabric pouches are easy to make or find online, and small padded cases can protect more fragile boards.
- If you're storing both your pendulum and board together, a dual-compartment case or pouch helps keep the two items secure and easy to access.

By crafting and using pendulum boards and mats, you expand the possibilities of your divination practice. These tools help organize and clarify pendulum readings, adding structure and depth to each session. Experiment with different designs, layouts, and materials to find or create a board that aligns with your unique needs and intentions. Once your board is ready, the next chapter will guide you in using your pendulum to ask specific questions, interpret responses, and deepen your intuitive connection with the guidance it provides.

Chapter 7: Crafting Pendulum Cases and Holders

Pendulums are delicate tools, and protecting them is essential for preserving both their physical condition and their energetic integrity. Crafting a pendulum case or holder allows you to create a safe, sacred space for your pendulum when it's not in use, protecting it from damage and unintentional energy interference. This chapter provides a guide on making cases from different materials, crafting display stands for ritual use, and personalizing cases to preserve and enhance your pendulum's energy.

Protecting Your Pendulum: Making Cases from Fabric, Wood, or Leather

A well-crafted case provides both physical protection and energetic shielding for your pendulum. The material you choose will affect its durability, appearance, and energy-holding properties, allowing you to customize a case that aligns with your style and needs.

1. **Fabric Cases:**
    - **Materials**: Soft fabrics like velvet, silk, cotton, or felt are ideal for pendulum cases. These materials are gentle on your pendulum's surface and offer a light, protective barrier.
    - **Crafting Steps:**
        - **Cut Fabric**: Cut two pieces of fabric, each about 6x3 inches, to create a small pouch. Adjust the size based on your pendulum's dimensions.
        - **Sew or Glue**: Place the pieces together with the outer sides facing inward, then sew or glue along the

sides and bottom, leaving the top open. Flip the fabric right-side out to hide the seams.

- **Drawstring or Flap**: Add a drawstring by folding over the top edge and sewing it down, then thread a ribbon or cord through to create a closing mechanism. Alternatively, you can add a small button or snap to secure the opening.

◦ **Decorative Touches**: Embroider symbols, initials, or patterns onto the fabric, or use fabric paint to personalize the case with designs that reflect your spiritual practice or intentions.

2. **Wooden Boxes**:

◦ **Materials**: Small wooden boxes, often available at craft stores, are ideal for sturdy pendulum cases. You can select boxes made of wood types known for their energetic qualities, such as oak (strength), cedar (protection), or pine (purification).

◦ **Crafting Steps**:

- **Prep and Sand**: Lightly sand the box to ensure a smooth surface.

- **Painting and Staining**: Choose wood stain or paint to add color and preserve the wood. Stains enhance the natural wood grain, while paint provides a customizable surface for intricate designs.

- **Lining the Interior**: Cut velvet, felt, or silk to fit the inside of the box. Secure the lining with glue, creating a cushioned bed to protect the pendulum from scratches.

◦ **Personalized Engravings**: Use a wood-burning tool or engraving pen to add symbols, such as a moon, sun, or sacred geometry, to the lid. Engraving personal symbols adds energy to the case, aligning it with your intentions for protection and sacredness.

3. **Leather or Suede Pouches**:
   - ◦ **Materials**: Leather or suede provides a luxurious, durable case for pendulums. You can use scraps or pre-cut leather sheets, often available in craft stores.
   - ◦ **Crafting Steps**:
     - ▪ **Cut Leather**: Cut a piece of leather large enough to wrap around your pendulum. You can create a simple envelope pouch or a cylindrical design.
     - ▪ **Sewing or Riveting**: For envelope-style pouches, fold the leather and sew the sides with a thick needle and waxed thread. For added durability, use rivets to secure the sides.
     - ▪ **Closure**: Use a leather cord to wrap around the pouch, or install a snap or button. For a rustic touch, add a bone, antler, or crystal bead as a decorative closure.
   - ◦ **Personalization**: Emboss symbols onto the leather by pressing stamps into it when the leather is slightly damp. You can create intricate designs using stamps of stars, moons, or runes, adding layers of personal symbolism.

Each material offers unique protective qualities: fabric pouches are soft and lightweight, wooden boxes are durable and grounding, and leather pouches are strong and weather-resistant. Choose the material that resonates with your style, durability needs, and energetic preferences.

Crafting Display Stands for Ritual Use

Displaying your pendulum on a stand not only showcases it beautifully but also holds it in a dedicated, sacred space when not in use. Display stands are especially useful if you incorporate your pendulum into a ritual space, altar, or meditation area.

1. **Wooden Display Stands**:
   - **Materials**: Use a small wooden base (like a circular or rectangular plaque) and a wooden dowel for the stand. You may also want to use decorative items like small hooks, beads, or crystals for added detail.
   - **Assembly Steps**:
     - **Attach the Dowel**: Drill a small hole in the base and insert the dowel, securing it with wood glue. The dowel should be tall enough to hang the pendulum from a small hook at the top.
     - **Add a Hook**: Attach a small hook or ring to the top of the dowel, which allows the pendulum to hang freely.
     - **Decoration**: Paint or stain the base and dowel, then add crystals, charms, or symbols to the base to infuse it with sacred energy.
   - **Symbolic Additions**: Consider adding symbols around the base, such as the moon phases, chakra symbols, or protective runes, to elevate the stand's sacred energy.
2. **Crystal and Stone Stands**:
   - **Materials**: For a more natural look, select a large crystal cluster (such as amethyst or quartz) or a flat stone slab as the base, combined with a thin metal rod or a wire loop for hanging.

- ◦ **Assembly Steps**:
    - ▪ **Attaching the Rod or Loop**: Use a strong adhesive or small drill to secure the rod or loop onto the crystal or stone slab.
    - ▪ **Display Options**: Drape the pendulum over the loop or place it directly on the crystal, allowing the stone's energy to cleanse and charge the pendulum when it's resting.
  - ◦ **Energetic Enhancements**: Choosing a specific crystal base, like selenite for cleansing or amethyst for spiritual connection, enhances the pendulum's energy when it's placed on the stand.

3. **Metal or Wire Display Stands**:
   - ◦ **Materials**: Use a wire frame or small metal stand, such as those used for jewelry displays or decorative items. You may need pliers and wire cutters to shape the metal.
   - ◦ **Assembly Steps**:
     - ▪ **Form the Stand**: Use wire to create a loop or spiral at the top of the stand, forming a place to hang the pendulum. The base can be a simple wire loop or a weighted object, like a stone.
     - ▪ **Decoration**: Wrap smaller decorative beads, crystals, or charms around the wire stand for added beauty and symbolic meaning.
   - ◦ **Benefits**: Metal stands offer a sleek, minimalist look and are sturdy for both large and small pendulums. They are also highly customizable, allowing you to mold the wire into unique shapes or forms.

Crafting a stand not only protects your pendulum from damage but also transforms it into a focal point in your sacred space. It creates a dedicated home for your pendulum when it's not in use and can serve as an altar piece or symbolic representation of your spiritual practice.

Personalizing Cases for Energy Preservation

A personalized case can enhance your connection to the pendulum and help preserve its energy between uses. By infusing the case with your intentions, symbols, and chosen colors, you create a space where your pendulum remains charged, protected, and energetically clear.

1. **Adding Energetic Symbols and Markings**:
   - Use symbols that hold personal or spiritual significance. These can be painted, embroidered, or engraved onto the case. Common symbols include:
     - **The Moon**: Represents intuition, guidance, and reflection. Ideal for pendulums used in spiritual readings.
     - **The Tree of Life**: Symbolizes growth, wisdom, and connection. This symbol is beneficial for grounding and connecting with ancestral energies.
     - **Sacred Geometry**: Patterns like the Flower of Life or Metatron's Cube can represent cosmic harmony and higher consciousness.
   - Adding these symbols transforms the case into a protective, sacred vessel, helping to maintain the pendulum's purity and alignment.
2. **Incorporating Colors for Intention**:
   - Choose colors that resonate with specific energies:
     - **Purple or Indigo**: Enhances intuition and spiritual awareness.
     - **Green**: Invites growth, balance, and healing.
     - **White or Silver**: Represents clarity and protection, ideal for cleansing and purity.
   - These colors can be incorporated through the case material itself, painted accents, or even embroidery threads.

3. **Embedding Crystals for Continuous Energy Cleansing**:
   - **Crystal Selection**: Small crystals, such as clear quartz, selenite, or black tourmaline, can be embedded in or attached to the case to provide continuous cleansing and protection.
   - **Placement**: Sew or glue crystals onto the inside or outside of the case. If using a wooden or leather case, drill a small hole to attach the crystals securely.
   - **Benefits**: Crystals like selenite cleanse energy continuously, while black tourmaline provides grounding and protection, ensuring that your pendulum remains energetically balanced and shielded.

4. **Adding Protective Herbs and Scents**:
   - Dried herbs like sage, lavender, or rosemary can be sewn into fabric cases to add protective and purifying qualities. Alternatively, you can place small sachets of herbs inside the case.
   - Essential oils, such as frankincense or sandalwood, can be applied sparingly to wood or leather cases for added protective energy. Use caution with oils on certain materials to prevent staining.
   - These additions help create an energetically sacred environment, preserving the pendulum's clarity and alignment.

5. **Infusing Your Case with Personal Intention**:
   - Hold the finished case in your hands, close your eyes, and set a specific intention for the case to protect, cleanse, and maintain your pendulum's energy. Visualize your intention filling the case, creating a sanctuary where your pendulum can rest and recharge.
   - Each time you place the pendulum in the case, take a moment to reconnect with this intention, reinforcing the protective and sacred nature of the case.

Crafting cases and holders for your pendulum allows you to maintain both its physical condition and its energetic purity, ensuring that it remains ready and aligned for your divination work. Through thoughtful material selection, creative designs, and personalized elements, you create a home that protects and nurtures your pendulum. By completing this chapter, you're now prepared to keep your pendulum safe and energetically clear, ready for the next stage of your divination practice. In the following chapter, you'll learn how to use your pendulum in various divination contexts, enhancing your readings with newfound confidence and connection.

Chapter 8: Using Your Pendulum for Divination

Using a pendulum for divination offers a simple yet profound way to tap into intuitive insights, gain clarity, and connect with subtle energies. While pendulums are well-suited for straightforward yes/no questions, they can also provide more complex insights and directional guidance. Learning to ask clear, focused questions and interpret the pendulum's responses will make your divination practice more effective and satisfying. In this chapter, you'll explore techniques for basic yes/no readings, directional readings, interpreting responses beyond simple answers, and framing questions to receive the most useful guidance.

Basic Yes/No and Directional Readings

Pendulums are commonly used to answer yes/no questions, offering quick insights and guidance with each swing. Mastering this basic skill provides a foundation for more advanced pendulum divination.

1. **Setting Up for a Yes/No Reading:**
   - Find a quiet space where you can sit comfortably and minimize distractions. Hold your pendulum by its chain or cord, allowing it to hang freely without touching any surfaces.
   - Take a few deep breaths, centering your mind and focusing your energy. Set an intention to receive clear, truthful guidance from your pendulum.
   - Before starting, establish the pendulum's specific signals for "yes," "no," and "maybe" or "uncertain." These re-

sponses can vary between individuals, so take time to calibrate your pendulum.

2. **Determining Yes, No, and Maybe Movements**:

   - Hold your pendulum steady and ask it to "Show me yes." Note the direction it moves—this could be a vertical swing, horizontal swing, or circular motion.

   - Next, ask it to "Show me no" and observe any change in direction. For example, if "yes" is a vertical swing, "no" might be a horizontal swing.

   - Lastly, ask it to "Show me maybe" or "Show me uncertain." This is typically a more ambiguous motion, like a slow or diagonal swing, indicating an unclear or inconclusive answer.

   - Practice these questions multiple times to ensure the pendulum consistently responds in the same way. Once you know its signals, you're ready to proceed with yes/no questions.

3.**Conducting a Yes/No Reading**:

   - Focus on a clear, straightforward question, such as "Is it in my best interest to attend this event?" or "Will I hear back about this job soon?" Keep your question specific, simple, and open-ended enough to allow for an unbiased response.

   - Hold the pendulum steady, ask your question aloud or mentally, and observe its movement. The pendulum should swing in the direction you've designated for "yes," "no," or "maybe."

   - If the pendulum's response is unclear or inconsistent, it could indicate an uncertain answer or suggest that the question needs reframing. Take a moment to refocus and try again, or rephrase your question to clarify its intent.

- **4.Directional Readings**:
  - Directional readings help you locate objects, gain insights about geographic areas, or guide decisions related to movement.
  - For example, you might ask, "Which direction should I take to find this item?" or "In which area should I focus my efforts today?"
  - Hold the pendulum over a compass or a surface where you can identify specific directions (e.g., north, south, east, west). As you ask the question, observe the pendulum's swing to see which direction it favors.
  - Be mindful that directional readings can be subtle, and it may take practice to interpret slight variations in the pendulum's motion.

Interpreting Responses Beyond Yes and No

While yes/no responses are common in pendulum divination, your pendulum can also provide more nuanced answers and insights. Learning to interpret these subtler responses will expand your ability to use the pendulum effectively.

1. **"Maybe" or "Uncertain" Responses**:
    - A "maybe" or "uncertain" response often occurs when the pendulum moves diagonally, wobbles, or swings with less intensity.
    - This response suggests that either the answer is not clear-cut, or the timing is not right for the question. It may also indicate that more information is needed before a decision can be made.
    - If you receive an uncertain answer, consider rephrasing the question to gain a clearer response, or revisit the question at a later time when conditions may have shifted.

2. **Intuitive Guidance in Ambiguous Responses**:
    - Sometimes, a pendulum's response might feel energetically "off," indicating that it is reflecting your own uncertainty or emotional state rather than a straightforward answer. In such cases, pause, center yourself, and ensure your mind is clear and calm.
    - Feel into the pendulum's movement intuitively—does it feel hesitant or resistant? Pay attention to your own inner responses to clarify whether the pendulum's motion is mirroring your internal state.

3. **Complex Answers Using an Alphabet or Number Layout**:
    - For more detailed questions, you can use a pendulum board with letters and numbers, allowing the pendulum to spell out words or indicate specific quantities.
    - Start with a simple question that requires more information, such as "What is the name of the person I need to

connect with?" or "How many weeks will it take for this project to be completed?"

- Hold the pendulum over the board and allow it to swing naturally, noting where it points. Be patient, as this process can be slower than a yes/no reading.
- Take notes as you go, especially if the pendulum is moving between multiple letters or numbers, and piece together the responses it provides.

4. **Reading Pendulum Speed and Intensity:**
   - In addition to direction, the speed and intensity of the pendulum's swing can convey additional layers of meaning. A strong, fast swing often indicates a clear or emphatic answer, while a slow, gentle swing might suggest a more tentative or nuanced response.
   - For example, a rapid "yes" response might indicate a strong affirmation or a sense of urgency, while a slower "no" could reflect hesitation or the need to proceed with caution.

5. **Yes/No Follow-Up Questions:**
   - To explore a question more deeply, use follow-up questions to build on a "yes" or "no" response. For example, if you receive a "yes" to "Should I consider this new job?" follow up with, "Is it likely to be fulfilling for me?" or "Will it support my long-term goals?"
   - Following up in this way allows you to add context and detail, creating a fuller picture from your pendulum's answers.

Asking the Right Questions to Get Clear Answers

The quality of your pendulum's responses often depends on the clarity and specificity of your questions. Asking the right questions ensures you receive answers that are both relevant and useful.

1. **Framing Clear, Direct Questions**:
   - Avoid vague or overly broad questions, as these can yield unclear responses. For example, instead of asking, "Will my life improve?" try a more specific question like, "Will focusing on self-care improve my emotional well-being?"
   - Aim for questions that have a straightforward answer, such as yes/no, timing, or directional guidance, especially when starting out with pendulum divination.

2. **Avoiding Emotionally Charged Questions**:
   - Emotional attachment can affect the pendulum's responses, as your own energy might influence its movement. If you're asking about a deeply personal or emotional issue, take a moment to center yourself and approach the question from a place of neutrality.
   - If you feel overly anxious or attached to a particular outcome, consider waiting until you are in a more balanced state before asking the question. Alternatively, ask an objective friend to assist in holding the pendulum for the reading.

3. **Using Open-Ended Follow-Up Questions**:
   - To expand on a simple yes/no answer, use open-ended follow-up questions. For instance, if you ask, "Is this the right time to start my project?" and receive a "yes," follow up with, "What is the best way for me to begin?" or "Are there specific resources I need?"

- Open-ended questions allow you to explore different aspects of the situation, adding depth to the pendulum's guidance.

4. **Rephrasing Ambiguous Questions**:
   - If you receive an unclear answer, try rephrasing the question for clarity. For instance, instead of asking, "Will I find love soon?" try asking, "Am I ready to attract a compatible partner?" or "Is there something I should focus on to attract a meaningful relationship?"
   - Rephrasing helps the pendulum respond to a more specific focus, especially if the original question was too broad or subjective.

5. **Testing Questions with Known Answers**:
   - When you're learning to ask the right questions, it's helpful to practice with questions to which you already know the answer. For instance, ask, "Is my name [Your Name]?" or "Is my birthdate in [Month]?" Testing the pendulum with known questions helps you build trust in its responses.
   - As your confidence grows, you can move on to questions that require new or unknown insights.

6. **Timing and Decision-Based Questions**:
   - For timing-based questions, ask about general time frames, such as "Will this event happen within the next three months?" or "Is it beneficial to act on this decision now?" Pendulums can be effective for timing questions if approached with a degree of flexibility.
   - With decision-based questions, break down complex decisions into smaller questions. Instead of asking, "Should I move to a new city?" consider questions like, "Will moving improve my career opportunities?" or "Is this the right time to move?"

Using a pendulum for divination opens a world of intuitive possibilities. By mastering yes/no and directional readings, interpreting responses beyond simple answers, and crafting clear, focused questions, you'll enhance the accuracy and reliability of your pendulum practice. Remember, the key to effective pendulum divination is a balanced combination of clarity, patience, and a strong connection to your own intuition. In the following chapter, you'll explore advanced pendulum techniques and practices that deepen your connection to this intuitive tool, expanding your ability to gain insight and guidance.

Chapter 9: Incorporating Pendulums into Daily Practice

Integrating your pendulum into daily life can turn it into a trusted ally for decision-making, personal guidance, and intuitive development. Using a pendulum regularly helps you build a stronger connection with it, making it a natural extension of your intuition. In this chapter, you'll explore how to use the pendulum for everyday decisions, ways to incorporate it into meditation and journaling, and practical exercises for enhancing your intuition and strengthening your bond with the pendulum.

Using the Pendulum for Decision-Making and Guidance

Pendulums are an excellent tool for receiving clear guidance and making everyday decisions, from small choices to significant life questions. They provide insight by tapping into your subconscious mind or universal energies, helping you approach decisions from a place of intuition rather than overthinking.

1. **Small Daily Decisions**:
    - Use your pendulum for simple questions related to everyday choices. For example, "Is it in my best interest to take this route to work today?" or "Would it be beneficial for me to attend this social event?" These questions are low-stakes and help you develop trust with your pendulum.
    - Approach small decisions with an open and curious mindset. By letting the pendulum guide minor choices, you become more comfortable relying on your intuition without overanalyzing.

2. **Career and Personal Development Decisions**:
   - For more significant choices, like career moves or personal development goals, break down the question into smaller components. For instance, instead of asking, "Should I accept this job offer?" try questions like "Is this job in alignment with my career goals?" or "Will this job support my personal growth?"
   - Take note of the pendulum's responses and ask follow-up questions if needed. Use the pendulum to clarify factors such as timing, location, or the job environment. Keep a journal to track your pendulum readings over time, especially if making decisions with lasting consequences.

3. **Decision-Making with Multiple Options**:
   - When faced with multiple options, create a pendulum board with labels for each choice or list them out in front of you, assigning each option a specific point on the board.
   - Ask the pendulum to guide you by pointing to the best option for your current situation. For example, if choosing between cities to move to, label each city on the board, then ask, "Which city would be most supportive of my personal growth and happiness?"
   - If the pendulum moves toward a specific point, consider it a recommendation. This approach works well for choices that involve multiple factors, as it gives a visual and structured way to let the pendulum guide you.

4. **Setting Boundaries and Empowered Choices**:
   - Pendulum readings are not about surrendering control; rather, they empower you to make informed, aligned choices. Always approach decisions with a sense of personal responsibility, using the pendulum as one component of your decision-making process.
   - Remember that you are the ultimate authority over your life, and pendulum guidance should feel like a gentle nudge

in the right direction rather than a rule. If you're unsure of a response, reflect on whether it resonates with your goals and values.

Integrating Pendulum Use into Meditation or Journaling

Combining pendulum use with meditation or journaling deepens your self-awareness and enhances the intuitive connection with your pendulum. These practices help you relax, clear your mind, and connect with the pendulum on a more spiritual level.

1. **Pendulum-Guided Meditation**:
   - **Purpose**: Use your pendulum to connect with inner guidance or set a theme for meditation. Begin by setting an intention, such as "What energy do I need to focus on today?" or "How can I cultivate more peace in my life?"
   - **Method**:
     - Sit quietly, hold your pendulum, and ask a question that aligns with your meditation goal.
     - Allow the pendulum to guide your focus. If it swings in a particular direction, let that be your meditative theme. For example, if it swings toward "yes," focus on affirming positive intentions; if it swings toward "no," focus on releasing unwanted thoughts or energy.
   - **Tips for Meditation**: Close your eyes, breathe deeply, and visualize the pendulum's response guiding you toward a peaceful, centered state. As thoughts arise, gently return to the pendulum's message, using it as a reminder of your purpose in the meditation.
2. **Using the Pendulum to Set Journaling Prompts**:
   - **Daily Reflection Prompts**: Ask the pendulum questions that inspire self-reflection, such as "What should I focus on today?" or "What lesson is waiting for me to discover?" Use

the pendulum's response to create journaling prompts, allowing it to guide your thoughts.

- ° **Exploring Emotions**: If you're feeling conflicted or unclear about a situation, ask the pendulum questions like "Am I holding onto unexpressed emotions?" or "Is there something I need to forgive?" Journal about the pendulum's answers to uncover deeper emotional insights.

- ° **Tracking Progress Over Time**: Use a separate journal to record daily pendulum readings and patterns. Over time, you may notice recurring themes or insights that reveal your growth, challenges, and areas where you're making progress.

3. **Creating a Pendulum-Focused Manifestation Ritual**:

- ° **Intentions and Affirmations**: Start by journaling your intention for something you wish to manifest in your life. Write down a clear affirmation, such as "I attract opportunities for growth and abundance."

- ° **Pendulum Validation**: Hold the pendulum and ask, "Is my intention in alignment with my highest good?" or "Will focusing on this intention benefit me?"

- ° **Daily Check-In**: Use the pendulum to guide small steps toward your manifestation goals. For example, "Is today a good day to take action on my intention?" Using it daily keeps your goals present in your mind and guides your progress.

Exercises for Enhancing Intuition and Connection

Your pendulum is more than a divination tool; it's also a bridge to your intuition. Practicing exercises that build your intuitive abilities strengthens your connection to the pendulum, allowing it to become more responsive to subtle insights and guidance.

1. **Daily Intuition Practice**:
    - **Exercise**: Set aside a few moments each day to use your pendulum as an intuitive check-in. Ask simple questions about your day, like "Will today be a productive day?" or "Is there anything I need to be aware of?"
    - **Self-Reflection**: After asking, take a few moments to tune into any intuitive feelings or impressions that arise. Note these thoughts, as they often align with the pendulum's response. Over time, this practice will help you trust your own instincts in addition to the pendulum's guidance.
2. **"Gut Feeling" Alignment Exercise**:
    - **Purpose**: Strengthen your intuitive responses by comparing your gut feelings with the pendulum's answers.
    - **Method**:
        - Before asking the pendulum a question, pause and note your initial instinct. What does your gut tell you?
        - Then, ask the pendulum the question and observe its response. Compare it to your initial feeling.
    - **Goal**: Notice where your intuition aligns with the pendulum's answers. This exercise helps you recognize patterns in your own intuition and teaches you when to trust your inner voice.
3. **Sensing Energy with the Pendulum**:
    - **Exercise**: Use the pendulum to sense the energy in various places, objects, or even people (with permission). For example, hold the pendulum over an object and ask, "Is this ob-

ject energetically aligned with me?" or "Does this space feel balanced and harmonious?"

- **Energy Check**: This exercise helps you become more aware of subtle energies around you, as well as the pendulum's responses to these energies. Practicing regularly will improve your ability to sense energy changes and environmental vibrations.

4. **Mindfulness and Centering Before Each Session**:

- Before using your pendulum, spend a few moments centering yourself with mindful breathing. Close your eyes, focus on your breath, and let any distracting thoughts dissolve.
- Visualize yourself becoming energetically aligned with your pendulum, creating a sense of unity. Practicing mindfulness enhances your connection to the pendulum, as a calm mind is better attuned to subtle shifts in energy and movement.

5. **Trust-Building Ritual with the Pendulum**:

- **Ritual**: Hold the pendulum, close your eyes, and set a clear intention to trust its guidance. Say an affirmation like, "I trust my pendulum to guide me with clarity and honesty."
- **Repetition**: Repeating this ritual daily strengthens the bond with your pendulum and reinforces your belief in its ability to reveal truthful guidance.
- **Result**: This trust-building exercise makes you more receptive to your pendulum's guidance, allowing it to become an integral part of your daily intuitive practice.

Incorporating your pendulum into daily life transforms it from a divination tool into a regular source of insight, support, and connection to your intuition. By using it for decision-making, integrating it into meditation and journaling, and practicing exercises to enhance your intuitive abilities, you strengthen your relationship with your pendulum and increase the clarity of its guidance. These practices build a foundation of trust and familiarity, allowing your pendulum to become a powerful companion in your journey of self-discovery and personal growth.

Appendices

Appendix A: Crystal Properties for Pendulum Use

Choosing the right crystal for your pendulum is an essential part of creating a tool that resonates with your specific intentions and spiritual needs. Each crystal carries unique energetic properties that can influence the pendulum's accuracy, responsiveness, and suitability for particular types of divination. In this appendix, we explore the properties of popular crystals for pendulum use, including their meanings, benefits, and ideal applications.

Amethyst: The Stone of Spirituality and Intuition

- **Color**: Purple to lavender
- **Chakra Association**: Third Eye (Ajna) and Crown (Sahasrara)
- **Properties**: Amethyst is known for its calming and spiritual properties, making it ideal for meditation, intuitive insights, and accessing higher consciousness. It enhances spiritual awareness, sharpens intuition, and promotes inner peace.
- **Uses in Pendulum Divination**: Amethyst pendulums are suitable for questions related to spiritual growth, emotional healing, and clarity. The stone's calming energy helps reduce anxiety, allowing you to approach divination with a clear and focused mind.

Rose Quartz: The Stone of Love and Compassion

- **Color**: Light pink to rose
- **Chakra Association**: Heart (Anahata)
- **Properties**: Rose quartz is associated with love, compassion, and emotional healing. It promotes self-love, empathy, and forgiveness, making it an ideal stone for exploring emotional questions.
- **Uses in Pendulum Divination**: Use a rose quartz pendulum for matters of the heart, such as relationships, self-acceptance, and emotional well-being. It's especially useful for questions related

to romantic or familial relationships and can help create a safe space for gentle, nurturing guidance.

Clear Quartz: The Master Healer and Amplifier

- **Color**: Transparent
- **Chakra Association**: All chakras, particularly the Crown (Sahasrara)
- **Properties**: Clear quartz is known for its ability to amplify energy and intention, making it one of the most versatile stones in divination. It enhances clarity, focus, and energy, amplifying both the pendulum's effectiveness and the user's intentions.
- **Uses in Pendulum Divination**: Clear quartz is an excellent all-purpose pendulum stone, suitable for a wide range of questions. It is especially beneficial for beginners, as it helps amplify clear answers and improves focus. Additionally, it can be programmed for specific intentions, making it a powerful choice for personalized divination.

Black Tourmaline: The Stone of Protection and Grounding

- **Color**: Black
- **Chakra Association**: Root (Muladhara)
- **Properties**: Black tourmaline is a grounding stone known for its protective qualities. It absorbs negative energy, shields against harmful influences, and promotes a sense of safety and stability.
- **Uses in Pendulum Divination**: Black tourmaline is ideal for energy-clearing work, boundary-setting, and readings where protection from outside influences is necessary. It is especially helpful when reading in potentially challenging environments or when seeking protection from emotional or psychic interference.

Citrine: The Stone of Abundance and Manifestation

- **Color**: Yellow to golden brown
- **Chakra Association**: Solar Plexus (Manipura) and Sacral (Svadhisthana)
- **Properties**: Citrine is associated with abundance, prosperity, and personal power. It fosters positivity, self-confidence, and motivation, making it an excellent choice for readings focused on career, financial decisions, and manifestation.
- **Uses in Pendulum Divination**: Citrine pendulums are ideal for questions related to success, confidence, and personal growth. It's a powerful stone for setting intentions and bringing clarity to questions of purpose, ambition, and financial prosperity.

Selenite: The Stone of Clarity and Spiritual Connection

- **Color**: White to translucent
- **Chakra Association**: Crown (Sahasrara) and Third Eye (Ajna)
- **Properties**: Selenite has a high vibrational frequency, offering a cleansing and purifying energy. It connects with higher consciousness and spiritual realms, making it a powerful tool for cleansing other crystals and amplifying intuitive abilities.
- **Uses in Pendulum Divination**: Selenite pendulums are best suited for spiritual inquiries, guidance from higher realms, and energy cleansing. Its clear energy allows for high levels of clarity, making it excellent for purification work and questions regarding spiritual growth.

Lapis Lazuli: The Stone of Wisdom and Truth

- **Color**: Deep blue with gold flecks
- **Chakra Association**: Third Eye (Ajna) and Throat (Vishuddha)
- **Properties**: Lapis lazuli is associated with wisdom, truth, and self-awareness. It enhances communication, intellectual insights, and inner vision, making it a great stone for exploring deep questions.
- **Uses in Pendulum Divination**: Use lapis lazuli for readings related to self-discovery, communication, and understanding hidden truths. This stone can be especially beneficial for exploring questions about personal growth, truth-seeking, and knowledge.

Obsidian: The Stone of Protection and Transformation

- **Color**: Black or deep brown
- **Chakra Association**: Root (Muladhara)
- **Properties**: Obsidian is a powerful grounding stone known for its protective and transformative energy. It assists in shadow work, healing emotional wounds, and releasing negative patterns.
- **Uses in Pendulum Divination**: Obsidian pendulums are well-suited for readings related to self-healing, emotional release, and protection. This stone's grounding energy can also assist in overcoming fears, uncovering hidden truths, and breaking free from old habits or patterns.

Moonstone: The Stone of Intuition and New Beginnings

- **Color**: Milky white with iridescent flashes
- **Chakra Association**: Third Eye (Ajna) and Sacral (Svadhisthana)
- **Properties**: Moonstone is known for enhancing intuition, emotional balance, and new beginnings. It resonates strongly with feminine energy and the cycles of the moon, making it ideal for exploring inner growth and transformation.
- **Uses in Pendulum Divination**: Moonstone pendulums are excellent for questions regarding cycles, intuition, and emotional healing. It's particularly helpful in divination for personal development, relationships, and transitions, as it brings insights that align with natural rhythms and changes.

Carnelian: The Stone of Vitality and Motivation

- **Color**: Red to orange
- **Chakra Association**: Sacral (Svadhisthana) and Solar Plexus (Manipura)
- **Properties**: Carnelian is associated with courage, motivation, and creative energy. It fosters enthusiasm, passion, and drive, making it ideal for energizing the spirit and enhancing focus.
- **Uses in Pendulum Divination**: Carnelian pendulums are ideal for questions about creativity, motivation, and overcoming personal blocks. It's a helpful stone for clarifying questions about one's life purpose, passion, and energy levels, especially in times of stagnation.

Smoky Quartz: The Stone of Grounding and Detoxification

- **Color**: Brown to smoky gray
- **Chakra Association**: Root (Muladhara)
- **Properties**: Smoky quartz is a grounding stone known for neutralizing negative energy and promoting emotional calm. It provides a stabilizing influence, helping to release unwanted attachments and reduce stress.
- **Uses in Pendulum Divination**: Smoky quartz pendulums are perfect for grounding and cleansing inquiries. This stone is especially useful in readings related to emotional release, stress relief, and stability, making it an ideal choice for questions about removing obstacles and creating balance.

Fluorite: The Stone of Mental Clarity and Focus

- **Color**: Green, purple, blue, or multicolored
- **Chakra Association**: Heart (Anahata) and Third Eye (Ajna)
- **Properties**: Fluorite is known for its ability to enhance mental clarity, focus, and organization. It brings a sense of calm and aids in decision-making, aligning well with intellectual and problem-solving work.
- **Uses in Pendulum Divination**: Fluorite pendulums are excellent for questions about clarity, learning, and decision-making. It's an ideal tool for students, researchers, or anyone seeking insight into complex matters or areas requiring concentration.

Labradorite: The Stone of Transformation and Psychic Abilities

- **Color**: Dark gray with flashes of blue, green, and gold
- **Chakra Association**: Third Eye (Ajna) and Crown (Sahasrara)
- **Properties**: Labradorite is known for its mystical, protective energy. It enhances psychic abilities, intuition, and transformation, making it suitable for exploration of hidden realms and deeper consciousness.
- **Uses in Pendulum Divination**: Labradorite pendulums are suited for divination involving change, spiritual insights, and psychic protection. This stone is perfect for exploring questions about one's life path, dreams, and metaphysical experiences.

Green Aventurine: The Stone of Luck and Opportunity

- **Color**: Green
- **Chakra Association**: Heart (Anahata)
- **Properties**: Green aventurine is known for attracting luck, abundance, and new opportunities. It has a soothing, optimistic energy that supports personal growth, making it ideal for manifesting prosperity.
- **Uses in Pendulum Divination**: Green aventurine pendulums are ideal for questions related to new beginnings, opportunities, and personal growth. Use it for guidance on financial decisions, career changes, or relationship matters that require a positive outlook.

This guide to crystal properties for pendulum use provides a starting point for selecting the ideal stone for your needs. Each crystal's unique qualities make it suitable for specific types of questions, from spiritual inquiries and emotional healing to practical guidance and manifestation. By choosing a crystal that aligns with your intentions, you create a

pendulum that becomes a highly personal tool for your divination journey.

Appendix B: Symbol Meanings for Pendulum Enhancements

Adding symbols to your pendulum, whether through charms, engravings, or beads, can deepen its power and resonance by aligning it with specific intentions and energies. Symbols have long been used in spiritual practices for their ability to convey complex ideas and embody particular energies. In this appendix, we'll explore the meanings of popular symbols and how they can enhance your pendulum, allowing you to personalize your tool for focused, intentional divination work.

The Tree of Life

- **Description**: The Tree of Life represents interconnectedness, growth, and wisdom. It appears in various cultures, symbolizing the eternal cycle of life, the union of earth and sky, and spiritual growth.
- **Meaning**: This symbol is connected to personal and spiritual growth, grounding, and connection to ancestry and universal knowledge.
- **Use in Pendulum**: Adding the Tree of Life enhances the pendulum's ability to connect with ancestral knowledge, provide wisdom, and guide questions related to one's life purpose, family roots, and personal development.

The Ankh

- **Description**: The Ankh is an ancient Egyptian symbol resembling a cross with a loop at the top, representing eternal life and the divine life force.
- **Meaning**: It is often associated with health, vitality, eternal life, and balance between the physical and spiritual realms.
- **Use in Pendulum**: Adding an Ankh to your pendulum empowers it with the energy of vitality and life-force connection, making it particularly useful for health-related questions, life purpose inquiries, and questions about achieving balance and vitality in life.

The Crescent Moon

- **Description**: The Crescent Moon symbolizes the lunar cycle, intuition, and feminine energy. It is often associated with mystery, intuition, and transformation.
- **Meaning**: The Crescent Moon represents growth, new beginnings, and the subconscious mind. It resonates strongly with intuition, dreams, and spiritual insights.
- **Use in Pendulum**: Enhancing your pendulum with the Crescent Moon strengthens its connection to intuition, making it ideal for spiritual inquiries, guidance on personal transformation, and deepening one's connection to the subconscious.

The Pentagram

- **Description**: The Pentagram is a five-pointed star within a circle, often used in pagan and Wiccan practices. Each point represents one of the five elements: earth, air, fire, water, and spirit.
- **Meaning**: It symbolizes protection, balance, harmony with nature, and the interconnectedness of all elements.
- **Use in Pendulum**: Adding a Pentagram enhances protection, grounding, and balance. This symbol is ideal for those seeking guidance in matters of personal harmony, energetic protection, and elemental alignment in their divination practice.

The Eye of Horus

- **Description**: An ancient Egyptian symbol representing protection, health, and power. It resembles an eye with markings that represent the markings of a falcon, linking it to the god Horus.
- **Meaning**: The Eye of Horus is a powerful symbol of protection, wisdom, and insight. It is used to ward off negative energies and enhance perception.

- **Use in Pendulum**: By incorporating the Eye of Horus, your pendulum gains protective qualities, as well as enhanced clarity and perception. This is beneficial for divination focused on truth-seeking, protection from negativity, and understanding hidden aspects of a situation.

The Om Symbol

- **Description**: The Om symbol is a sacred sound and spiritual icon in Hinduism and Buddhism, representing the essence of the universe.
- **Meaning**: It symbolizes universal consciousness, harmony, and spiritual awakening. Om is considered the primordial sound from which all creation emerged.
- **Use in Pendulum**: Adding the Om symbol enhances the pendulum's connection to universal energy, aiding in spiritual enlightenment and questions of higher consciousness. It's especially powerful for meditation, spiritual guidance, and inner peace.

The Spiral

- **Description**: The Spiral is an ancient symbol that appears in various cultures, symbolizing cycles, evolution, and life's journey.
- **Meaning**: The Spiral represents growth, transformation, and the cyclical nature of life. It's often associated with personal evolution, renewal, and connection to natural rhythms.
- **Use in Pendulum**: Incorporating the Spiral enhances the pendulum's alignment with natural cycles and personal growth. This symbol is ideal for divination focused on change, transformation, and aligning with life's natural flow.

The Hamsa Hand

- **Description**: The Hamsa is a hand-shaped symbol with an eye in the center, traditionally used in Middle Eastern cultures to ward off the "evil eye" and bring protection.
- **Meaning**: It symbolizes protection, good fortune, and blessings. The eye in the Hamsa wards off harmful energies and enhances intuition.
- **Use in Pendulum**: The Hamsa Hand enhances protection and positive energy, making it suitable for readings where safeguarding oneself or focusing on blessings is important. It adds a layer of spiritual shielding to the pendulum, making it an excellent choice for psychic protection during divination.

The Lotus Flower

- **Description**: The Lotus Flower is an important symbol in many Eastern religions, symbolizing purity, enlightenment, and rebirth, as it grows in muddy water but emerges clean.
- **Meaning**: It represents spiritual growth, purity, resilience, and enlightenment. The lotus teaches about rising above challenges and staying connected to one's divine nature.
- **Use in Pendulum**: Adding the Lotus Flower to your pendulum strengthens its ability to provide insight during challenging times. It's a powerful enhancement for questions about spiritual growth, resilience, and finding peace amid adversity.

Sacred Geometry (Flower of Life, Seed of Life)

- **Description**: Sacred geometry patterns like the Flower of Life or Seed of Life are complex geometric shapes that represent the fundamental patterns of creation.
- **Meaning**: Sacred geometry symbolizes harmony, balance, and the interconnectedness of all life. These symbols are thought to contain powerful spiritual wisdom.
- **Use in Pendulum**: Incorporating sacred geometry enhances the pendulum's alignment with universal laws and harmony. This is ideal for readings about purpose, alignment with higher truths, and understanding one's place within the larger universe.

Feathers

- **Description**: Feathers are associated with air, freedom, and communication, and often represent messages from the spirit world.
- **Meaning**: Feathers symbolize spiritual messages, guidance, freedom, and lightness of spirit. They are thought to be signs from guides or higher realms.
- **Use in Pendulum**: Adding a feather charm enhances communication with spirit guides or higher realms. It's perfect for readings involving guidance from the spiritual world, understanding divine messages, and gaining clarity on matters of the soul.

The Sun

- **Description**: The Sun symbolizes life, vitality, and enlightenment. It is a universal symbol of energy, growth, and positive power.
- **Meaning**: The Sun represents clarity, optimism, success, and warmth. It brings life-giving energy and is associated with confidence and joy.

- **Use in Pendulum**: Adding a Sun charm or engraving enhances positive energy, motivation, and clarity. It's an excellent symbol for questions about personal empowerment, growth, and success, as well as for providing guidance in times of change or challenge.

The Infinity Symbol

- **Description**: The Infinity symbol (∞) is a mathematical sign that represents something without an end. Spiritually, it signifies eternity and the interconnectedness of all things.
- **Meaning**: It symbolizes continuity, boundless possibilities, and unity. The infinity symbol reminds us of life's ongoing cycles and eternal nature.
- **Use in Pendulum**: Incorporating the Infinity symbol into your pendulum emphasizes wisdom, continuity, and spiritual connection. It's a meaningful addition for readings related to life purpose, cycles, and understanding the "big picture."

The Triskelion (Triple Spiral)

- **Description**: The Triskelion, or triple spiral, is an ancient Celtic symbol representing progress, cycles, and the triad of life (birth, life, death).
- **Meaning**: This symbol signifies personal growth, forward movement, and cycles of renewal. It is often associated with the elements and life's transformative journey.
- **Use in Pendulum**: The Triskelion enhances the pendulum's alignment with personal evolution, making it ideal for divination involving change, growth, and forward movement. It can help you gain insight into where you are in life's cycles and how to move toward your next phase.

The Yin-Yang

- **Description**: The Yin-Yang symbol from Chinese philosophy represents duality and balance, symbolizing the harmonious co-existence of opposite forces.
- **Meaning**: It signifies balance, duality, and harmony between light and dark, feminine and masculine, and passive and active energies.
- **Use in Pendulum**: Adding the Yin-Yang symbol promotes balance and harmony, making it ideal for readings where balance is needed, such as in relationships, health, or emotional well-being. It helps the pendulum provide answers that align with a balanced, harmonious outcome.

By understanding and choosing the right symbols to enhance your pendulum, you can create a tool that aligns more closely with your personal intentions, spiritual path, and divination goals. Whether it's for protection, clarity, connection to universal energy, or personal growth, each symbol adds a unique layer of meaning, amplifying your pendulum's energy and enhancing its effectiveness in guiding you on your journey.

Currently we have tarot mats on the makingplaycards.com/apophisoccultshopBottom of Form

Qr code down below.

Appendix C: Troubleshooting and Common Questions

Even with regular practice, pendulum use can sometimes lead to uncertain or confusing results. Understanding common issues, knowing how to troubleshoot effectively, and being aware of frequently asked questions can enhance the accuracy and reliability of your pendulum readings. In this appendix, we cover common troubleshooting steps, solutions for erratic responses, and answers to frequently asked questions.

Troubleshooting Common Issues

1. **Pendulum Swings Erratically or Doesn't Move at All**
   - **Possible Cause**: Erratic movement or lack of response can be due to interference from your energy, a cluttered mental state, or environmental influences.
   - **Solution**:
     - **Clear Your Mind**: Take a few deep breaths, close your eyes, and try to center yourself. Anxiety or mental distractions can cause instability in pendulum movement. Visualize calm energy flowing from your hand to the pendulum.
     - **Cleansing the Pendulum**: Cleanse your pendulum to clear any residual energies that might be affecting its motion. Common cleansing methods include smoke cleansing, placing it in moonlight, or using a selenite charging plate.
     - **Environmental Check**: Move to a quieter space if you're surrounded by noise or other distractions.

Check for drafts or fans that might be interfering with the pendulum's movement.

2. **Inconsistent Yes/No Responses for the Same Question**
   - **Possible Cause**: Inconsistent answers can occur if the question is poorly phrased, emotionally charged, or if there's a lack of clarity in your intention.
   - **Solution**:
     - **Clarify the Question**: Rephrase the question to make it more specific and direct. Avoid ambiguous language and ensure that the question has a straightforward yes or no answer.
     - **Check for Emotional Bias**: If you're emotionally attached to a specific answer, it can subconsciously influence the pendulum's movement. Take a moment to center yourself and let go of any attachment to the outcome before asking again.
     - **Give It Time**: Some questions may require time to develop a clear answer. If you receive mixed responses, wait and return to the question at a later time.

3. **The Pendulum Gives a "Maybe" or "Uncertain" Answer Repeatedly**
   - **Possible Cause**: A repeated "maybe" or "uncertain" answer can indicate that the timing isn't right for the question, or that more information is needed.
   - **Solution**:
     - **Ask Follow-Up Questions**: Clarify the original question by breaking it down into smaller parts or asking for further guidance. For example, "Is there something I need to understand before proceeding?"
     - **Reflect on Timing**: Some questions may not have clear answers because conditions are still unfolding. If you're asking about future events, try rephrasing

the question to focus on the present moment or revisit the question later.

- **Consider Alternative Tools**: If the pendulum consistently responds with "maybe" or "uncertain," consider using a different divination tool, such as tarot cards or meditation, to gain additional insight.

4. **Pendulum Responds Slowly or with Minimal Movement**
   - **Possible Cause**: Minimal or slow movement can indicate low energy, either in the environment or from the user, or that the pendulum needs cleansing or recharging.
   - **Solution**:
     - **Re-Energize**: Charge the pendulum by placing it in sunlight, moonlight, or on a crystal like clear quartz or selenite for a few hours.
     - **Recenter Yourself**: Ground your energy by taking deep breaths or performing a brief meditation. Ensure you are calm and balanced before beginning your session.
     - **Check Your Energy Levels**: Fatigue or emotional stress can impact the pendulum's responsiveness. If you're feeling drained, try using the pendulum at a later time when you feel more energetic.

5. **Pendulum's Directional Responses Change Over Time**
   - **Possible Cause**: Sometimes, pendulums change their yes/no signals due to energetic shifts in the user or environment. It can also happen if the pendulum wasn't "calibrated" or attuned consistently.
   - **Solution**:
     - **Re-Calibrate the Pendulum**: Spend a few moments asking the pendulum to show you its current "yes," "no," and "maybe" responses. Note any changes and continue using those directions as the pendulum's new default.

- **Regular Calibration Practice**: Before each session, quickly check your pendulum's yes/no signals. This keeps the connection consistent and avoids confusion in readings.

6. **Physical Factors Interfering with the Pendulum's Movement**
    - ○ **Possible Cause**: Drafts, fans, uneven surfaces, or even hand strain can affect the pendulum's movement.
    - ○ **Solution**:
        - **Environmental Adjustments**: Move to a place where air currents are minimal. Ensure you're holding the pendulum in a stable position with your elbow supported, if needed, for extra control.
        - **Holding Technique**: Hold the pendulum lightly but steadily, avoiding excessive tension. A relaxed grip will allow for smoother and more natural movement.

Common Questions and Their Answers

1. **How Often Should I Cleanse My Pendulum?**
   - **Answer**: Cleanse your pendulum whenever you feel it may have absorbed unwanted energy, if it's been used by others, or after particularly intense readings. Regular cleansing can be performed weekly or monthly, depending on your usage frequency and preference. Cleansing after each use can be beneficial if you use your pendulum for different types of questions or in varied environments.

2. **Can I Use the Same Pendulum for Different Types of Questions?**
   - **Answer**: Yes, most pendulums can be used for different types of questions, from practical matters to spiritual inquiries. However, if you feel that your pendulum resonates better with specific topics (e.g., relationships, career, spiritual growth), you may choose to dedicate it solely to those questions. Some people have multiple pendulums for different purposes, but this is a personal choice.

3. **What Should I Do if I'm Emotionally Attached to a Particular Outcome?**
   - **Answer**: If you feel emotionally invested in a specific answer, take a few moments to center yourself and release attachment to the outcome. Approach the question with a sense of openness. If you're struggling to remain neutral, ask a friend to hold the pendulum for the reading or wait until you feel less emotionally charged.

4. **Can I Use a Pendulum During Difficult Emotional States?**
   - **Answer**: It's generally best to use a pendulum when you're calm and centered. Strong emotions like anger, anxiety, or grief can influence the pendulum's response and lead to unclear or biased answers. If you're experiencing intense

emotions, consider grounding exercises, meditation, or journaling before turning to your pendulum for guidance.

5. **How Can I Improve My Connection with the Pendulum?**
   - **Answer**: Strengthen your connection with regular practice, mindfulness, and intention-setting. Spending a few minutes each day holding your pendulum, meditating with it, or using it for small decisions helps build trust. You can also personalize the pendulum by adding charms or symbols, dedicating it to specific purposes, or practicing gratitude for its guidance.

6. **Can I Let Others Use My Pendulum?**
   - **Answer**: Allowing others to use your pendulum is a personal decision. Some people are comfortable with others using their pendulum, while others feel it can disrupt the energetic connection. If someone else uses your pendulum, cleanse it afterward to remove any residual energies and reset it to your own energy.

7. **Is It Normal for My Pendulum to Change Its Responses Based on My Mood?**
   - **Answer**: Yes, your mood and energy can influence your pendulum's responses. This is why it's important to approach readings with a calm and neutral mindset. Practicing grounding and centering techniques before a session can help stabilize responses, reducing the effect of mood swings on the pendulum's movement.

8. **How Do I Know if My Pendulum Is Giving Me Accurate Answers?**
   - **Answer**: Accuracy comes with practice, intention, and maintaining a clear mental state. Try testing your pendulum with known questions to observe its response patterns, and trust that consistency will build over time. Keep a journal to track the accuracy of past readings, and remember that practice and self-reflection improve reliability.

9. **Can I Use My Pendulum to Ask Future-Oriented Questions?**

   ◦ **Answer:** Pendulums can provide insights into future possibilities, but it's important to remember that the future is influenced by many variables and free will. Approach future-oriented questions as guidance rather than definite predictions. For example, ask, "Is this likely to happen if I continue on my current path?" rather than expecting a fixed outcome.

10. **What if I Can't Decide Between Two or More Options?**

    ◦ **Answer:** When choosing between options, assign each option a specific location on your pendulum board or create a mental map. Ask the pendulum to indicate the most beneficial choice based on your current situation. If you still feel unsure, consider breaking down the question into smaller components or exploring each option through follow-up questions.

11. **How Can I Use a Pendulum to Confirm My Intuition?**

    ◦ **Answer:** Before consulting your pendulum, take a moment to connect with your own intuitive feelings or gut instincts about a situation. Note what you feel or think, and then ask the pendulum to confirm or clarify your intuition. This practice reinforces your trust in both your intuition and your pendulum's guidance, creating a harmonious balance between inner knowing and external confirmation.

12. **Why Does My Pendulum Sometimes Stop Working Altogether?**

    ◦ **Answer:** Pendulums can stop responding for various reasons, such as energetic blockages, fatigue, or the need for a break. If this happens, cleanse and recharge your pendulum and take a break from divination. Reflect on whether you may be over-relying on the pendulum for answers or if there's an emotional blockage that needs addressing before proceeding.

By understanding common troubleshooting techniques and being mindful of these frequently asked questions, you can create a smoother, more effective pendulum practice. Each question and solution provides deeper insight into how to interact with your pendulum in a way that respects both its energy and your own, allowing you to build a consistent, reliable divination tool.

Appendix D: Rituals and Exercises for Pendulum Users

Incorporating rituals and exercises into your pendulum practice deepens your connection with this divination tool and strengthens your intuition. Rituals help set intentions, cleanse and energize the pendulum, and create a sacred space for your divination work. Exercises, on the other hand, enhance your skill, trust, and intuitive abilities. This appendix provides detailed rituals and exercises to help you build a meaningful and powerful pendulum practice.

Rituals for Pendulum Users

1. **Pendulum Consecration Ritual**
   - **Purpose**: To dedicate and energize a new or existing pendulum, aligning it with your specific intentions and spiritual energy.
   - **Materials**: Your pendulum, a small candle (white or purple), incense (such as sage, sandalwood, or frankincense), a small bowl of salt, and a crystal (such as clear quartz).
   - **Steps**:
     - **Create a Sacred Space**: Begin by setting up a small altar or a quiet space. Light the candle and incense to create a calm atmosphere.
     - **Cleanse the Pendulum**: Hold your pendulum over the smoke from the incense, saying, "I cleanse this pendulum of any energy that does not serve my highest good." Then, sprinkle a few grains of salt over the pendulum to further purify it.
     - **Set an Intention**: Hold the pendulum in your hands and close your eyes. Focus on your intention for the pendulum—whether it's guidance, clarity, or protection—and say, "I consecrate this pendulum to be a source of truth, clarity, and wisdom in my life."
     - **Charge with Crystal Energy**: Place the pendulum on the clear quartz or another crystal, letting it rest

there for a few moments to absorb the crystal's energy.

- **Close the Ritual**: Extinguish the candle and give thanks to the energies present. Keep the consecrated pendulum in a special place, as it's now aligned with your purpose.

2. **Morning Pendulum Energy Alignment Ritual**
   - **Purpose**: To align the pendulum with your energy at the beginning of each day, ensuring it's clear and responsive for the day's readings.
   - **Materials**: Your pendulum, a selenite or amethyst crystal, and a quiet space.
   - **Steps**:
     - **Center Yourself**: Take a few deep breaths and focus on your intention for the day.
     - **Align and Cleanse**: Place the pendulum on the selenite or amethyst for a few minutes to cleanse and recharge it.
     - **Hold and Set Intentions**: Hold the pendulum in your hand, close your eyes, and say an affirmation such as, "Today, may this pendulum be a clear guide, in alignment with my highest good and my purpose."
     - **Thank and Use**: After setting your intention, give thanks, and carry the pendulum with you for daily questions or guidance.

3. **Full Moon Cleansing and Charging Ritual**
   - **Purpose**: To deeply cleanse and recharge your pendulum using the moon's energy, especially during the full moon, when energies are heightened.
   - **Materials**: Your pendulum, a small bowl of water (optional), and an outdoor or window space exposed to moonlight.

- ◦ **Steps**:
  - ▪ **Cleanse in Water**: (Optional) If your pendulum's material allows, gently dip it in a bowl of water, saying, "I cleanse this pendulum of all accumulated energies."
  - ▪ **Place in Moonlight**: Set the pendulum on a windowsill or outside, where it can be bathed in moonlight overnight. Visualize the moon's light purifying and charging it.
  - ▪ **Intention Setting**: Close your eyes and set an intention, such as, "Under the full moon, may this pendulum absorb clarity, truth, and alignment with universal energies."
  - ▪ **Retrieve in the Morning**: Collect the pendulum in the morning, feeling its refreshed energy. Full moon rituals are particularly powerful for resetting and re-energizing the pendulum for the month ahead.

4. **Grounding and Centering Ritual Before Readings**
   - ◦ **Purpose**: To ground yourself and create a clear mental and energetic state before using the pendulum for divination.
   - ◦ **Materials**: A small grounding stone (such as hematite or black tourmaline) and your pendulum.
   - ◦ **Steps**:
     - ▪ **Breathe and Center**: Sit comfortably, holding the grounding stone in one hand and the pendulum in the other. Take a few deep breaths, focusing on releasing any tension.
     - ▪ **Visualize Rooted Energy**: Imagine roots growing from your feet into the ground, anchoring you and creating stability. Visualize any scattered energy flowing down into the earth.

- **Set Your Intention**: Say aloud, "I am grounded, centered, and connected to my highest truth. May this pendulum guide me with clarity and wisdom."
- **Begin Reading**: With a calm and clear state, begin your pendulum reading, trusting in the guidance that follows.

Exercises for Enhancing Intuition and Connection

1. **Daily Yes/No Practice**
   - **Purpose**: To develop a strong, consistent connection with your pendulum and refine your ability to interpret yes/no responses accurately.
   - **Exercise**:
       - Choose a time each day to ask your pendulum simple yes/no questions, preferably ones with known answers, like "Is my name [Your Name]?" or "Is today [the correct day of the week]?"
       - Observe the pendulum's movements, noting the consistency of its yes/no signals.
       - Track your responses in a journal to monitor patterns. Over time, you'll build confidence and consistency with your pendulum's movements.
2. **Intuitive Questioning Exercise**
   - **Purpose**: To practice asking questions intuitively and developing a natural flow with your pendulum's responses.
   - **Exercise**:
       - Sit quietly with your pendulum and ask an open-ended question, such as, "What energy is surrounding me today?" or "Is there something I need to focus on right now?"
       - Allow your pendulum to respond with "yes," "no," or directional swings. Follow up by asking clarifying

questions based on its movements, letting your intuition guide the next questions.

- Reflect on any insights gained during the exercise and record your experiences. This practice will strengthen your ability to let intuition lead your pendulum work.

3. **Pendulum and Crystal Chakra Alignment Exercise**
   - **Purpose**: To use your pendulum for balancing and aligning the chakras, enhancing both intuitive awareness and energetic health.
   - **Exercise**:
     - Lay down comfortably and hold your pendulum over each chakra point, starting from the root and moving upward to the crown.
     - Ask your pendulum, "Is this chakra balanced?" Observe its movement. If it swings steadily, the chakra is likely in balance; if it wobbles or moves inconsistently, it may indicate an imbalance.
     - For any imbalances, visualize each chakra in its corresponding color, imagining it spinning in a harmonious rhythm. After visualizing, ask your pendulum if the chakra has balanced, noting any changes.
     - Complete the exercise feeling refreshed and grounded. This practice enhances both energetic balance and your ability to sense subtle shifts.

4. **Pendulum Journaling and Reflection Exercise**
   - **Purpose**: To use journaling alongside pendulum readings for deeper self-reflection and personal growth.
   - **Exercise**:
     - Begin each journaling session by holding the pendulum and asking a question about personal insight, such as, "What lesson is most important for me today?" or "What energy should I embrace this week?"

- Write down the pendulum's response and your thoughts. Reflect on how the guidance applies to your current life situation.
- Throughout the week, check back on the guidance received to see how it unfolds. This exercise builds a habit of integrating pendulum insights into daily life.

5. **Energy Sensitivity Exercise with Objects**
   - **Purpose**: To practice using your pendulum to sense energy in various objects, improving your energetic sensitivity and connection to the pendulum.
   - **Exercise**:
     - Select a variety of objects around your home—crystals, plants, jewelry, and even water. Hold the pendulum over each object and ask, "Is this item energetically aligned with me?"
     - Observe the pendulum's movement, noting the variations in responses. For example, a positive energy match might lead to a strong swing, while a neutral or low-energy match might result in minimal movement.
     - Keep a record of the objects tested and the pendulum's responses. Over time, you'll become more adept at sensing the subtle energies of various objects and strengthening your sensitivity.

6. **Dream Guidance Exercise**
   - **Purpose**: To receive insights from your dreams by using your pendulum to guide dream intention and interpretation.
   - **Exercise**:
     - Before bed, ask your pendulum, "Is there something I need to know through my dreams tonight?" Note the response.

- Set an intention to remember any dreams upon waking, and keep a notebook nearby.
- In the morning, write down any dreams you recall. Use your pendulum to ask clarifying questions about specific dream symbols or messages, such as, "Does this symbol represent my current emotional state?" or "Is this dream relevant to a specific situation in my life?"
- This practice deepens your connection to both your subconscious mind and your pendulum, allowing insights to surface through both dreams and divination.

By practicing these rituals and exercises regularly, you'll deepen your relationship with your pendulum, build confidence in your abilities, and enhance your intuitive skills. Each practice brings you closer to the pendulum as an extension of your intuition, helping you incorporate this sacred tool into your daily life with greater intention and clarity. Whether you're seeking daily guidance, self-awareness, or energetic balance, these rituals and exercises provide a pathway to a profound, meaningful pendulum practice.

<u>Message from the Author:</u>

I hope you enjoyed this book, I love astrology and knew there was not a book such as this out on the shelf. I love metaphysical items as well. Please check out my other books:

-Life of Government Benefits

-My life of Hell

-My life with Hydrocephalus

-Red Sky

-World Domination:Woman's rule

-World Domination:Woman's Rule 2: The War

-Life and Banishment of Apophis: book 1

-The Kidney Friendly Diet

-The Ultimate Hemp Cookbook

-Creating a Dispensary(legally)

-Cleanliness throughout life: the importance of showering from childhood to adulthood.

-Strong Roots: The Risks of Overcoddling children

-Hemp Horoscopes: Cosmic Insights and Earthly Healing

- Celestial Hemp Navigating the Zodiac: Through the Green Cosmos

-Astrological Hemp: Aligning The Stars with Earth's Ancient Herb

-The Astrological Guide to Hemp: Stars, Signs, and Sacred Leaves

-Green Growth: Innovative Marketing Strategies for your Hemp Products and Dispensary

-Cosmic Cannabis

-Astrological Munchies

-Henry The Hemp

-Zodiacal Roots: The Astrological Soul Of Hemp

- **Green Constellations: Intersection of Hemp and Zodiac**

-Hemp in The Houses: An astrological Adventure Through The Cannabis Galaxy

-Galactic Ganja Guide

Heavenly Hemp
Zodiac Leaves
Doctor Who Astrology
Cannastrology
Stellar Satvias and Cosmic Indicas
<u>Celestial Cannabis: A Zodiac Journey</u>
AstroHerbology: The Sky and The Soil: Volume 1
AstroHerbology:Celestial Cannabis:Volume 2
Cosmic Cannabis Cultivation
The Starry Guide to Herbal Harmony: Volume 1
The Starry Guide to Herbal Harmony: Cannabis Universe: Volume 2

Yugioh Astrology: Astrological Guide to Deck, Duels and more
Nightmare Mansion: Echoes of The Abyss
Nightmare Mansion 2: Legacy of Shadows
Nightmare Mansion 3: Shadows of the Forgotten
Nightmare Mansion 4: Echoes of the Damned
The Life and Banishment of Apophis: Book 2
Nightmare Mansion: Halls of Despair
<u>Healing with Herb: Cannabis and Hydrocephalus</u>
<u>**Planetary Pot: Aligning with Astrological Herbs: Volume 1**</u>
Fast Track to Freedom: 30 Days to Financial Independence Using AI, Assets, and Agile Hustles
<u>**Cosmic Hemp Pathways**</u>
How to Become Financially Free in 30 Days: 10,000 Paths to Prosperity
Zodiacal Herbage: Astrological Insights: Volume 1
Nightmare Mansion: Whispers in the Walls
The Daleks Invade Atlantis
Henry the hemp and Hydrocephalus

10X The Kidney Friendly Diet
Cannabis Universe: Adult coloring book

Hemp Astrology: The Healing Power of the Stars

Zodiacal Herbage: Astrological Insights: Cannabis Universe: Volume 2

<u>Planetary Pot: Aligning with Astrological Herbs: Cannabis Universes: Volume 2</u>

Doctor Who Meets the Replicators and SG-1: The Ultimate Battle for Survival

Nightmare Mansion: Curse of the Blood Moon

<u>The Celestial Stoner: A Guide to the Zodiac</u>

Cosmic Pleasures: Sex Toy Astrology for Every Sign

Hydrocephalus Astrology: Navigating the Stars and Healing Waters

Lapis and the Mischievous Chocolate Bar

Celestial Positions: Sexual Astrology for Every Sign

Apophis's Shadow Work Journal: : A Journey of Self-Discovery and Healing

Kinky Cosmos: Sexual Kink Astrology for Every Sign

Digital Cosmos: The Astrological Digimon Compendium

Stellar Seeds: The Cosmic Guide to Growing with Astrology

Apophis's Daily Gratitude Journal

Cat Astrology: Feline Mysteries of the Cosmos

The Cosmic Kama Sutra: An Astrological Guide to Sexual Positions

Unleash Your Potential: A Guided Journal Powered by AI Insights

Whispers of the Enchanted Grove

Cosmic Pleasures: An Astrological Guide to Sexual Kinks

369, 12 Manifestation Journal

Whisper of the nocturne journal(blank journal for writing or drawing)

The Boogey Book

Locked In Reflection: A Chastity Journey Through Locktober

Generating Wealth Quickly:

How to Generate $100,000 in 24 Hours

Star Magic: Harness the Power of the Universe

The Flatulence Chronicles: A Fart Journal for Self-Discovery

The Doctor and The Death Moth

Seize the Day: A Personal Seizure Tracking Journal

The Ultimate Boogeyman Safari: A Journey into the Boogie World and Beyond

Whispers of Samhain: 1,000 Spells of Love, Luck, and Lunar Magic: Samhain Spell Book

Apophis's guides:

Witch's Spellbook Crafting Guide for Halloween

<u>Frost & Flame: The Enchanted Yule Grimoire of 1000 Winter Spells</u>

<u>The Ultimate Boogey Goo Guide & Spooky Activities for Halloween Fun</u>

Harmony of the Scales: A Libra's Spellcraft for Balance and Beauty

The Enchanted Advent: 36 Days of Christmas Wonders

Nightmare Mansion: The Labyrinth of Screams

Harvest of Enchantment: 1,000 Spells of Gratitude, Love, and Fortune for Thanksgiving

The Boogey Chronicles: A Journal of Nightly Encounters and Shadowy Secrets

The 12 Days of Financial Freedom: A Step-by-Step Christmas Countdown to Transform Your Finances

Sigil of the Eternal Spiral Blank Journal

A Christmas Feast: Timeless Recipes for Every Meal

Holiday Stress-Free Solutions: A Survival Guide to Thriving During the Festive Season

Yu-Gi-Oh! Holiday Gifting Mastery: The Ultimate Guide for Fans and Newcomers Alike

Holiday Harmony: A Hydrocephalus Survival Guide for the Festive Season

Celestial Craft: The Witch's Almanac for 2025 – A Cosmic Guide to Manifestations, Moons, and Mystical Events

Doctor Who: The Toymaker's Winter Wonderland

Tulsa King Unveiled: A Thrilling Guide to Stallone's Mafia Masterpiece

If you want solar for your home go here: https://www.harborsolar.live/apophisenterprises/

Get Some Tarot cards: https://www.makeplayingcards.com/sell/apophis-occult-shop

<u>Get some shirts: https://www.bonfire.com/store/apophis-shirt-emporium/</u>

<u>Instagrams:</u>
@apophis_enterprises,
@apophisbookemporium,
@apophisscardshop
Twitter: @apophisenterpr1 Tiktok:@apophisenterprise
Youtube: @sg1fan23477, @FiresideRetreatKingdom
Hive: @sg1fan23477
Podcast: Apophis Chat Zone: https://open.spotify.com/show/
5zXbrCLEV2xzCp8ybrfHsk?si=fb4d4fdbdce44dec

Newsletter: https://apophiss-newsletter-27c897.beehiiv.com/

Get printable holiday budget planners: apophisenterprises-llc.org/Apophis-emporium-shop /ols/products/holiday-budgeting-packageprintable

www.ingramcontent.com/pod-product-compliance
Lightning Source LLC
Chambersburg PA
CBHW011953170726
47994CB00025B/3282